Printed by C Hullmandel

A K E .

New Bond St Dec.r 1823

JOSEPH KISHERE

and the

MORTLAKE POTTERIES

Frontispiece. *Photograph from a coloured lithograph by Charles King c.1830. A horse-drawn barge in the foreground is featured against the river frontage of Mortlake on the bend of the Thames. A malt house and two oast houses are in evidence.*

JOSEPH KISHERE
and the
MORTLAKE
POTTERIES

Jack Howarth and Robin Hildyard

ANTIQUE COLLECTORS' CLUB

Dedicated to the memory of
the late Leslie Freeman
Formerly archivist to the
Barnes and Mortlake History Society

ISBN 1 85149 462 6

British Library Cataloguing-in-Publication Data
A catalogue record for this book is available from the British Library

The publication of this book would not have been possible
without a generous grant from
Ceramica-Stiftung, Basel, Switzerland.

Printed in China
by the Antique Collectors' Club Ltd., Woodbridge, Suffolk

Antique Collectors' Club

THE ANTIQUE COLLECTORS' CLUB was formed in 1966 and quickly grew to a five figure membership spread throughout the world. It publishes the only independently run monthly antiques magazine, *Antique Collecting*, which caters for those collectors who are interested in widening their knowledge of antiques, both by greater awareness of quality and by discussion of the factors which influence the price that is likely to be asked. The Antique Collectors' Club pioneered the provision of information on prices for collectors and the magazine still leads in the provision of detailed articles on a variety of subjects.

It was in response to the enormous demand for information on 'what to pay' that the price guide series was introduced in 1968 with the first edition of *The Price Guide to Antique Furniture* (completely revised 1978 and 1989), a book which broke new ground by illustrating the more common types of antique furniture, the sort that collectors could buy in shops and at auctions rather than the rare museum pieces which had previously been used (and still to a large extent are used) to make up the limited amount of illustrations in books published by commercial publishers. Many other price guides have followed, all copiously illustrated, and greatly appreciated by collectors for the valuable information they contain, quite apart from prices. The Price Guide Series heralded the publication of many standard works of reference on art and antiques. *The Dictionary of British Art* (now in six volumes), *The Pictorial Dictionary of British 19th Century Furniture Design*, *Oak Furniture* and *Early English Clocks* were followed by many deeply researched reference works such as *The Directory of Gold and Silversmiths*, providing new information. Many of these books are now accepted as the standard work of reference on their subject.

The Antique Collectors' Club has widened its list to include books on gardens, garden design, garden history and architecture. All the Club's publications are available through bookshops world wide and a full catalogue of all these titles is available free of charge from the addresses below.

Club membership, open to all collectors, costs little. Members receive free of charge *Antique Collecting*, the Club's magazine (published ten times a year), which contains well-illustrated articles dealing with the practical aspects of collecting not normally dealt with by magazines. Prices, features of value, investment potential, fakes and forgeries are all given prominence in the magazine.

Among other facilities available to members are private buying and selling facilities and the opportunity to meet other collectors at their local antique collectors' club. There are over eighty in Britain and more than a dozen overseas. Members may also buy the Club's publications at special pre-publication prices.

As its motto implies, the Club is an organisation designed to help collectors get the most out of their hobby: it is informal and friendly and gives enormous enjoyment to all concerned.

For Collectors — By Collectors — About Collecting
ANTIQUE COLLECTORS' CLUB
www.antique-acc.com

Sandy Lane, Old Martlesham, Woodbridge, Suffolk, IP12 4SD, UK
Tel: 01394 389950 Fax: 01394 389999
e-mail: sales@antique-acc.com
or
Eastworks, 116 Pleasant Street - Suite ≠60B, Easthampton, MA 01027
Tel: (413) 529 0861 Fax: (413) 529 0862 Orders: (800) 252 5231
e-mail: info@antiquecc.com

Molt House   Mortlake Church   Queens Head   Mortlake   Pottery

CONTENTS

Above and opposite above. Plates 1 and 1a. *Riverside views of Mortlake (Plate 1) and Vauxhall (Plate 1a) from a book entitled* Mortlake and the Thames *and described as:* The Panorama of the Thames from London to Richmond. Exhibiting every object on both banks of the river with a general description of the most remarkable places and a general view of London. Published by Samuel Leigh, 18 Strand. *The book is undated but was probably published c.1825 – Sanders' pottery was closed in 1823 and the property remained empty until some date after 1830 when it was converted to a malthouse.* COURTESY OF THE LOCAL STUDIES LIBRARY, RICHMOND UPON THAMES

Plate 2. *An enlarged detail from Plate 1 (Mortlake). The building on the left is described as a pottery although it is equipped with ventilators typical of oast houses and the bottle oven projecting through the roof of the factory on the extreme right is undoubtedly a potter's kiln, identifying Sanders' potworks. The pyramidal structures fronting the premises to the left of the pottery are malt kilns, part of a malthouse.*

CONTENTS

Plates 3 and 3a. *A coloured drawing of the Nine Elms windmill is found in the* Panorama of the Thames *from London to Richmond (Plates 1 and 1a refer) which is dated to c.1825. The windmill, occupied by Sanders & Crisp in the mid-18th century, was sited at the water's edge on the side of a creek, the outlet of the River Effra into the Thames. It also features the Vauxhall pottery, founded in 1683 by John de Wilde, another link with Mortlake, William Wagstaff having worked the pottery from 1793 to 1802 before moving his business to Sanders' Mortlake pottery.*

ILLUSTRATIONS AND PLANS

AUTHORS' PREFACE

This book brings together the writings and research of Robin Hildyard, Jack Howarth and the late John Eustace Anderson to provide a fascinating and definitive history of a small but important Mortlake pottery established by Joseph Kishere in the late eighteenth century. It tells of his relationship, as a former employee, with the larger potworks founded by John Sanders fifty years earlier in the same Thames-side village and, whilst giving coverage to the Sanders operation, the prime focus is of course on the working life of Joseph Kishere and his stoneware products. The word 'definitive' is used here with diffidence, surmising that a gem of new information may well turn up at any time in the future.

Plate 4. *Caricature of Sir Brook Watson in his late sixties. A hand coloured etching by Robert Dighton 1803.*

If we include John Eustace Anderson, each of the three contributors to this work brings a different but complementary perspective to the subject, and each shares a common fund of historical data which is reflected in their writings. Anderson's book *A Short Account of the Mortlake Potteries* (Appendix 7) was published in 1894, some fifty years after the closure of both potteries. His material relied heavily on the fading memories of local residents, in particular one or two surviving members of the Kishere family, perhaps explaining some of the inaccuracies in his work.

Combining an artistic, commercial and historical approach, Robin Hildyard's 'Stoneware' section gives a comprehensive overview of the English salt glaze potteries and identifies Joseph Kishere's niche in a very competitive market. The style and range of his products, from the origin of the potworks to the final closure, are described in detail and fully illustrated.

The third contribution, from Jack Howarth, takes a different approach. This provides an insight into the history of the Kishere pottery by tracing Joseph Kishere's ancestry back to the earliest contacts between his father, Benjamin, and John Sanders when both families resided in Lambeth. A description of eighteenth century Mortlake, the village in which Joseph Kishere lived and worked, sets the scene for the development of his modest enterprise.

Plate 5. *A stoneware bottle inscribed 'Topham'.* **Sanders** *factory, mid-18th century. H. 9in. (23cm).*

One of the attractions of Kishere wares to serious stoneware collectors was the proprietor's willingness to mark some, but not all, of his output with his surname or initials. Whilst certain distinctive features on marked examples can be useful in identifying unmarked pieces, Joseph's close connection with the Sanders works does create areas of uncertainty in correctly attributing wares between the two Mortlake potteries.

Interestingly, in describing and illustrating the decorative sprigging on Kishere products, there are many references to the ever popular 'Punch Party', said by some commentators to be based on Hogarth's 'Midnight Modern Conversation'. In fact the earliest use of the plaque on a London stoneware mug was in 1729, some two years earlier than the Hogarth painting and three years earlier than the print of 1732/3. Hogarth's print is a parody of Dutch tavern scenes by Jan Steen and others, a more likely source of the original inspiration for the 'Punch Party' plaque, but the popularity of Hogarth's print no doubt contributed later to the various versions used on London stonewares.

Josiah Wedgwood, Thomas Minton and Josiah Spode are but three well-remembered names from a host of entrepreneurs who collectively established the British ceramics industry by the end of the eighteenth century. All three commenced business producing earthenware tablewares, subsequently adding decorative lines and porcelain to their range, and all were alive to and enriched by the benefits of mass production techniques. Their employees were counted in hundreds – by 1819 Spode's factory employed about eight hundred workers. Deservedly, the major players in this nascent industry have been well researched and comprehensively documented in numerous excellent books. By contrast the Mortlake potteries can in no way be compared with the industrialised giants of the Midlands and, never having produced tableware and never becoming a household name, their history has been given only limited attention by ceramic historians. Nevertheless, they made a unique contribution to English brown stonewares, bridging the very different worlds of the eighteenth and nineteenth centuries, and the authors' twofold aim is to update and expand the story and to bring Joseph Kishere's role to a far wider audience.

J.A.H.
R.J.C.H.

ACKNOWLEDGEMENTS

Tracing the ancestry of Joseph Kishere could not have been accomplished without the support of the late Leslie Freeman who kindly provided copy extracts from the Mortlake Churchyard and Cemetery listings and readily helped in disentangling the conflicting evidence gathered from a variety of sources. His death in March 2000 was a sad loss to his family, his many friends and the members of the Barnes and Mortlake History Society, their valued archivist for many years.

From the outset David Thomas has been a willing volunteer, giving invaluable support in proof-reading everything from first drafts to final proofs. His amendments and improvements to the text have always been gratefully received.

There are very few published works on the subject of ceramics which do not include an acknowledgement of the assistance given by Rodney Hampson and this book is no exception. Having been of enormous help in editing an earlier history of *Andrew Abbott and the Fleet Street Partnerships* he suggested that Thomas Abbott of Richmond upon Thames may be related. A connection remains unproven but the research led directly to Joseph Kishere's potworks in Mortlake and once again Rodney Hampson was ready with technical information and suggestions for which we are greatly indebted.

There is a vast amount of information available in the Local Studies Room of the Richmond upon Thames Library and during many months of research Jane Baxter, the archivist, was extremely helpful and uncomplaining in producing documents, prints and dealing with innumerable enquiries.

John Fisher at The Guildhall Library introduced their computerised information system known as 'Collage' which provides quick and easy access to over 30,000 images including 6,000 paintings, watercolours etc. from the Guildhall Art Gallery and more than 25,000 prints, drawings, maps etc. from the Library's Print Room.

Advice from Nigel Forbes-Marsden, with his knowledge of Thames navigation, was very welcome and whilst he may not have invented the down-draught kiln he was adept at illustrating its principles.

There has been no lack of help from many archives and museums including The National Art Library (Kensington), The Public Record Office (Kew), The General Register Office (Kingsway), The Surrey History Centre (Woking) and The Lambeth Archives (Minet Library, Lambeth). Special thanks are due to Lynn Miller at The Wedgwood Museum, Barlaston and Miranda Goodby of The Potteries Museum & Art Gallery, Stoke-on-Trent for their generous assistance.

The search for illustrations of Kishere/Mortlake wares involved some special people: Edwina Ehrman, Keeper of Decorative Arts at the Museum of London, Susan Lunt, Curator of Decorative Arts (Ceramics) at the National Museum and Galleries on Merseyside, Stella Beddoe, Keeper of Decorative Art, Brighton Museum and Art Gallery, Jonathan Horne, BADA President and specialist in early English pottery, Kensington Church Street, London, John Goulding, a stoneware collector, Leslie Spatt in the Parish Office of St. Mary's Church, Mortlake and Lynne Broadbent for providing much needed help in preparing the index.

Most research depends in some measure on what has gone before. In the case of Mortlake, we owe a great debt to the foresight of John Eustace Anderson in writing his *Short Account of the Mortlake Potteries* at a time when Kishere's pottery was still remembered by local inhabitants. Since then the subject has been kept alive by J.F. Blacker's *ABC of Salt-glazed Stoneware* (1922), the Faber Monograph by A. Oswald, R.J.C. Hildyard and R.G. Hughes *English Brown Stoneware* (1982), the V & A catalogue *Browne Muggs* (1985), Jonathan Horne's exhibition catalogue of 1985 and the papers given by Dr. David Redstone to the English Ceramic Circle and to Morley College Ceramic Circle. Many collections have provided examples of Mortlake stoneware for study, notably the Woolley Collection at the Minet Library, the Struan Robertson Collection at Brighton Museum, the Victoria & Albert Museum, the Museum of London, and the collection of the late Robert Hill of Windlesham.

~ Chapter One ~

MORTLAKE AND THE THAMES

The University Boat Race ensures that Mortlake, on the south bank of the River Thames, is not a forgotten conurbation of Greater London. As long as it remains the finishing post for this major sporting event there will be an annual reminder accompanied with fleeting, media pictures but, as we shall see, Mortlake also has many historical reasons for remaining in our memories.

Leslie Freeman in his excellent record of the Mortlake Parish Church[1] gives a thumbnail sketch of some prominent residents, most of whom are commemorated by memorials in the church. From this list we can select three titled gentlemen with interesting and contrasting personalities who were living in the village when Joseph Kishere was operating his High Street pottery. Joseph would be aware of them at least by name, probably through the church, and there can be little doubt that they would be familiar with Joseph's salt glaze works.

Sir Philip Francis (1740-1818) resided in Mortlake from 1783 to 1805. At school he proved to be a good classical scholar and became captain at St. Paul's School, but despite

Plate 6. The two tankards have similar decoration with a central plaque of the 'Punch Party', two riders, a beater and hounds chasing a stag. Left. Plated mount. H. 8in.(20.3cm). c.1800, probably **Kishere.** *Right. Sheffield plated mount and glass base. H.8¼in.(21cm). c.1800, probably* **Kishere.**

a propitious start he never completely fulfilled his ambitions, due probably to his arrogance and vindictiveness. On leaving school in 1756 he was employed as a junior clerk in the Secretary of State's Office and towards the end of 1762 moved to a more senior post as first clerk at the War Office where he remained until 1772. His biographer, Joseph Parkes, attempts to link Francis' name with Junius, a pseudonym adopted by the author of innumerable vitriolic letters published in the press ferociously attacking royalty, statesmen and government policies. This correspondence may or may not have been the handiwork of Francis but, if it was, as a government employee in the War Office he would have needed to preserve absolute anonymity.

In 1774, two years after leaving the War Office, he was assigned to a government post in India, leaving his wife and six children in England. Earlier, Warren Hastings, formerly the Governor of Bengal, became the Governor-General of India, reflecting the expansion of British colonial interests in the subcontinent, and in his new role was to be supported

Plate 7. *Left. One gallon jug with Sheffield plate mount. The sprigging includes a plaque of the two boors drinking, a post-windmill, a hunter with dog and gun and a mounted lady and gentleman with hounds chasing a stag. H. 13in. (33.1cm), c.1795-1800,* **Mortlake.** *Left foreground. Gill jug decorated with rider, beater and dogs chasing a hare. H.4¼in. (10.8cm), c.1790-1800,* **Mortlake.** *Right. Tankard featuring a plaque of the 'Punch Party', classical figures and two riders with hounds chasing a stag. H. 7½in. (19.1cm), c.1800,* **Kishere.** *Centre. Quart jug with a plaque of the 'Punch Party', tree sprigs, huntsman with dog and gun and a rider and dogs chasing a fox. H. 7in. (17.7cm), c.1800, probably* **Kishere.**
COURTESY OF JONATHAN HORNE ANTIQUES LTD., KENSINGTON CHURCH STREET

and controlled by a council of four of which Francis was appointed a council member. Sir Philip's years in India can be described as colourful – his affair with a beautiful sixteen year old lady, who also happened to be the wife of an officer of the East India Company, ended in discovery, humiliation and a fine of 50,000 rupees. This incident was followed by a disagreement with Warren Hastings which, together with references to Francis' private conduct revealed in official papers, resulted in a duel. He quickly recovered from a severe bullet wound and departed from India at the end of 1780 having amassed a fortune, partly from gambling. He was none too popular on returning to London.

Between 1784 and 1807, the dates virtually coinciding with his residence in Mortlake, he served as a Member of Parliament for various constituencies and whilst he was never regarded as a good speaker he was a staunch supporter of the Whig party. His overriding ambition to be appointed Governor-General of India following the death of Cornwallis in 1805 was not achieved and the honour of a knighthood may not have been adequate compensation. He retired from parliamentary life in 1807 and lived in St. James's Square, London for some thirteen years prior to his death.

To our modern eyes Sir Brook Watson (1735-1807) would have cut a strange figure as he walked along Threadneedle Street to the Bank of England where he ultimately became Deputy Governor. It was to be many years before artificial limbs were perfected and in the eighteenth century an unsightly wooden leg (Plate 4) was the only answer to the loss of a lower limb. Unfortunately Watson suffered this cruel fate at the early age of fourteen when he was attacked by a shark while bathing at Havana (Plate 8). His early days may not have been much happier. Born in 1735 he was left an orphan only six years later and brought up by an aunt. According to one source[2] 'about 1749 he was sent to America to join a relative in business at Boston' (an English settlement in Massachusetts since 1630). A second source[3] does not quote a date but states that 'he went to sea' and implies that he joined a ship shortly after leaving school at age twelve or thirteen. The two versions are not incompatible and he could have spent a short time as a sailor before the move to Boston.

His brief maritime experience and his association with, if not involvement in, the Boston business must have been invaluable training for his future career. Anglo-French rivalry over territorial claims in Canada had reached breaking point in the 1750s and Watson happened to be in the right place at the right time. In 1755 he served as commissary under Colonel Robert Monckton at the siege of Beausejour, situated near the present-day Winnipeg, and in 1758 as commissary under Wolfe who captured the French fortress of Louisbourg on Cape Breton, a strategic site defending the entrance to the St. Lawrence River. It is known that Brook Watson was awarded civil contracts to procure supplies and provisions for these military campaigns. Such contracts, which may have included the supply of seamen and shipping, are known to have been highly profitable and they no doubt helped him to finance the launch of a business partnership in Halifax, Nova Scotia (1758) and a London business, trading to America, in partnership with a John Mauger (1759). Trade with America, with or without partners, continued for at least fifteen years and the biographical notes mention that Watson was in America just before the outbreak of the Revolution where he acted as a secret service agent before coming back to England in 1775.

Plate 8. *Watson and the shark, 1778. Oil on canvas by John Singleton Copley RA (1738-1815). A descriptive panel accompanying the painting reads: 'This picture representing a remarkable occurrence in the life of Brook Watson was bequeathed to the Royal Hospital of Christ in London by his will. He was of a very good family in the north of England but having lost both his parents early in life was brought up by an aunt, and before the age of fourteen years manifested a strong predilection for the sea, which led to the misfortune represented in this picture. He served in the Commissariat Department of the army under the immortal Wolfe at Louisberg [sic] in 1758. In 1759 he was established as a merchant in London, and was subsequently called upon to act as Commissary General to the army in America commanded by Sir Guy Carleton, late Lord Dorchester. On his return from that service he was elected as Alderman of the City of London and one of its representatives in Parliament, and continued member of the House of Commons till he was appointed to the situation of Commissary General to the Army under His Royal Highness the Duke of York, acting on the continent of Europe. In 1796 he was chosen Lord Mayor, and in 1803 created a baronet of the United Kingdom. He died in 1807 an Alderman of the City of London, deputy governor of the Bank of England, &C. &C. To activity and exertion are the sources of public and private virtue and the road to honours and respect. The picture was painted by John Singleton Copley Esq. Royal Academician in the year 1778'.*

The following list of his subsequent appointments exemplifies a man of exceptional energy whose impressive career was achieved despite his physical handicap:

1779   Had a leading involvement in the formation of a corps of light horse volunteers used in the Spring of 1780 to help in the suppression of riots protesting against an Act of 1778 which repealed some of the anti-Roman Catholic legislation still embodied in statute law. The uprising was led by Lord George Gordon, head of the Protestant Association, and the rioters held London at their mercy for nearly a week, engaging in an orgy of murder and destruction.

1782-1783   Served as Commissary General of Canada under Sir Guy Carleton.

1784-1807   With the exception of a three year break (1793-1795★) he was a director of the Bank of England throughout this period and served as Deputy Governor in the last two years from 1806 to 1807.

1784-1807   Alderman for the Cordwainer Ward in the City of London.

1784-1793   Member of Parliament for London. Not unexpectedly he took a considerable interest in Canadian and Newfoundland affairs and in the supply of seamen and shipping.

1785-1786   Sheriff for the Cordwainer Ward.

1790-1791   Master of the Musicians' Company.

1793-1795★ Commissary General to the Duke of York's army. This was Britain's first expeditionary force to the Continent following the outbreak of the Napoleonic Wars.

1796-1797   Lord Mayor of London.

1796-1806   Chairman of Lloyds.

1798-1806   Commissary General for Great Britain.

1803   Created a baronet.

In contrast to Sir Philip Francis, the ill luck of Watson's early life was turned into a successful career and he was described by Lord Liverpool as 'one of the most honourable men ever known'. It is difficult to reconcile such high praise with the unkind caricature of Watson in his late sixties and also the 'broadside' included in Appendix 4 which is an interesting but feeble attempt to mar his election prospects. He took up residence in East Sheen, Mortlake in 1780 and died there in 1807.

A former Prime Minister, Henry Addington (1757-1844), was another noted resident of Mortlake where he is buried and commemorated in the church. Addington's education included Winchester, Lincoln's Inn and Oxford University from where he graduated in 1778 with a B.A. degree. He studied law for a number of years and, influenced by his close friend William Pitt, turned to politics, becoming the Member of Parliament for Devizes in 1784. As a parliamentarian he devoted himself to committee work and House of Commons' procedures, making him an ideal candidate for the office of Speaker which he occupied with great distinction for eleven years from 1789.

A political disagreement between Pitt and the King brought a reluctant Addington to power at a critical stage in the Napoleonic Wars. Continuing unrest in Ireland together with the perceived threat of invasion by Bonaparte 'through the Irish back door' persuaded Pitt that a solution was imperative and in 1801 the Act of Union received approval in both Houses of Parliament. Pitt calculated that a single parliament with English, Scottish and Irish Protestants would ensure a permanent majority over the Irish Papists. To achieve this it was also necessary to revise the oath of allegiance which excluded Catholics both from Parliament and supreme office. However, George III refused to break the coronation oath in which he swore to protect the Protestant Constitution. Pitt's offer of resignation was accepted and at the king's invitation Addington agreed to form a new government.

Arthur Bryant[4] describes Addington as a 'weak, well-meaning, inexperienced mediocrity ... He was merely a stop-gap. His cabinet of second-rate peers and sons of peers contained no one who commanded the slightest confidence except the sailor, St. Vincent'. Shortly after taking office his new administration made informal overtures for peace which were contemptuously rejected by Bonaparte. However, within a few weeks the situation had changed as a result of two British victories, one naval and the other military. In the first, at the Battle of Copenhagen, Nelson overpowered the Danish fleet and its floating batteries thereby removing any threat of naval intervention from the Baltic League, an anti-British coalition instigated by Napoleon and formed by Russia, Sweden and Denmark. A few days before Nelson's success, a victory on land was achieved by Abercromby against the French army based in Egypt which subsequently opened the way to Cairo and the conquest of that country.

Following these reversals Napoleon, not surprisingly, became more amenable to at least a temporary respite and England, after eight years of war, also needed peace. Addington's administration reopened negotiations and lengthy, tortuous discussions finally produced the Treaty of Amiens signed in March 1802. The armed forces were immediately placed on a peacetime footing but Addington's trust in Napoleon was completely misplaced and only fourteen months later the policy of appeasement was in tatters. War with France resumed in May 1803 and the government embarked on an urgent programme of rearmament. Confidence in Addington's leadership collapsed, leading to his resignation in April 1804 and the restoration of Pitt as Prime Minister. Shortly after leaving office Addington was created Viscount Sidmouth, an honour which did not signify the end of his political career. His principal assignment came in 1812 when he was appointed Secretary of the Home Department in Lord Liverpool's administration, a post which he held for ten years and, contrary to his usual kindly nature, one in which he was resolutely severe in dealing with any rioting or lawlessness.

Sidmouth's residence in Mortlake dates from 1801 to the year of his death in 1844, George III having given him possession of the White Lodge in Richmond Park, Mortlake at the time of his appointment as Prime Minister.

The brief histories of Sir Philip Francis, Sir Brook Watson and Lord Sidmouth help to bring colour and life to the village in the late eighteenth and early nineteenth centuries when Mortlake, a mere nine miles upstream from London, was an ideal country retreat for gentlemen and their families wishing to escape the less desirable aspects of living in the capital. In a wider context, Watson's involvement in Canadian affairs and Sir Philip's posting to India are reminders of a fast growing Empire which, following the defeat of Napoleon, would make Britain the dominant world power of the nineteenth century. As the Empire expanded so the commercial opportunities grew and the exploitation of these new markets helped to negate Bonaparte's closure of all Continental ports to British ships. Addington, when Prime Minister, briefly presided over a fourteen month armistice in the war with France which had lasted over twenty years. Against this historical and commercial background the Mortlake potters lived, worked and prospered.

Mortlake owes its limited growth to the proximity of the capital's large and rapidly expanding market, not forgetting the important commercial artery provided by the Thames, the river meandering southerly from Kew and a mile or so downstream sweeping in a northerly direction towards Hammersmith. Mortlake lies on the south bank at the southern extremity of the loop (Plate 9). The phrase 'limited growth' is used deliberately in that Mortlake, including East Sheen, is bounded to the south by Richmond Park, to the north by the Thames and is further constrained to west and east by Richmond and Putney respectively, both being faster growing communities. The table below illustrates the population growth of these areas and for comparison includes the Lambeth figures as an indication of London's rapid expansion.

	Acres	Year	Population	% Increase	Density/Acre
Putney	2,280	1801	2,428		
		1841	4,684	93%	2.05
Barnes	820	1801	860		
		1841	1,461	70%	1.78
Richmond	1,230	1801	4,628		
		1841	7,760	68%	6.3
Mortlake	1,910	1801	1,748		
		1841	2,778	59%	1.45
Lambeth	3,640	1801	27,985		
		1841	115,888	say 300%	31.8

In addition to the geographical constraints, Mortlake's area of 1,910 acres included 640 acres of Richmond Park which severely restricted residential and commercial development. Of the remaining 1,270 acres, in excess of 400 were devoted to horticulture and farming according to the Survey of 1811 (Appendix 2).

As with so many English hamlets and villages the first positive reference to Mortlake in historical records is to be found in the Domesday survey of 1086 which names this established Saxon village as 'Mortlage' and reads:

The Archbishop holds in demesne Mortlage. In the time of King Edward it was assessed at 80 hides. The Canons of St. Paul's hold 8 of these hides, which were included in that assessment; and they are now rated together at 25 hides. The arable land consists of 35 carucates. Five carucates are in demesne; and there are eighty villeins, and fourteen bordars, with 28 carucates.

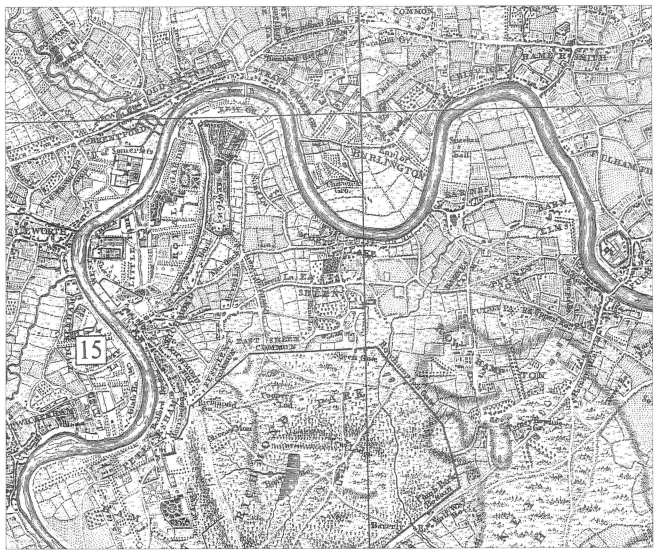

Plate 9. A detail from Rocque's map of London, dated 1746, showing Mortlake's location on the River Thames and its relationship to Richmond, Richmond Park and Putney. Transport links to the north of the Thames were enhanced by the bridge from Putney to Fulham and later by Kew Bridge, opened in 1759 but only at the 'proposed stage' when this map was drawn. COURTESY OF THE GUILDHALL LIBRARY, CORPORATION OF LONDON

There is a church; and sixteen bondmen; and two mills worth 100 shillings; and 20 acres of meadow. The wood yields 55 swine for pannage.– There are [belonging to this manor] in London 17 houses, paying 52 pence; in Southwark, 4 houses, paying 27 pence; and from the vill of Putelei, 20 shillings toll; and one fishery not rated: this fishery Earl Harold held in Mortlage, in the time of King Edward, and Stigand the archbishop held it a long while in the reign of William; yet they say that Harold erected it by force in the land of Chingestune and that of the Canons of St. Paul's. The whole manor in the time of King Edward, was valued at 32 pounds, afterwards at 10 pounds, and now at 38 pounds.

If the Domesday scribes had realised that historians and students would be referring to their work some nine hundred years later they would surely have added a glossary defining some of the unfamiliar terminology! A carucate (or hide) is thought to have represented an area of approximately 120 acres. If so the 68 carucates and 20 acres of meadow, totalling 8,180 acres (roughly 13 square miles), closely resembles the 8,710 acres quoted in 1801 as the combined acreage for Mortlake, Wimbledon, Putney and Barnes, the four parishes of the ancient manor of Mortlake.

Domesday was never intended to be a population census and, apart from bondmen, only ninety-four individuals are mentioned although they are the heads of the households and the figure does not include family members. Opinions differ but multiples of four or five, giving theoretical populations of 376 and 470, are not unreasonable. If the bondmen and church personnel are added the Mortlake manor had an estimated population of four to five hundred.

Mortlake is just one example of some nine thousand manors, situated principally in the Midlands and southern counties, and by good fortune a tithe map of Mortlake dated 1838 still exists. It delineates the archaic medieval strips forming part of a furlong which in turn was a sub-division of a commonfield. Gradually villagers commuted their feudal services and dues into money payments, establishing a landlord and tenant relationship and opening the way for the acquisition of neighbouring land by the more ambitious farmers. The creation of fields enclosed by hedges and areas devoted to horticulture was proceeding apace well before the Enclosure Acts of the 1750s which simply accelerated the process.

In the course of time Mortlake became an important market garden centre supplying fresh produce to the fast-expanding London market. Sir Richard Phillips, when visiting the area in the 1810s, was impressed by the scale of cultivation and made specific reference to 'Penley, the Mortlake gardener, who had occupied his grounds since the Restoration'.[5] The name of Richard Penley is to be found in the 1811 Survey (Appendix 2) where he is described as a market gardener cultivating ten acres of which four acres are rented and we can readily picture a conversation with Sir Richard Phillips in which Penley proudly stated that he and his ancestors had worked the land since Charles II was restored to the throne 160 years earlier. In fact Penley's holding was modest compared with other Mortlake growers mentioned in the Survey, including John Biggs with 146 acres, mostly rented; John Hope owning 48 acres, partly covered with hothouses and greenhouses; and William Grayson cropping 39 acres of rented land.

At one time Mortlake was noted for the quantity of its lavender and asparagus. London's rudimentary sanitation in the eighteenth century must have created a strong demand for lavender and William Grayson is said to have made a fortune from growing asparagus. C. Marshall Rose[6] quotes an apposite paragraph from Cassell's *Topographical Guide to the County of Surrey:*

> Great quantities of vegetables and fruit are grown for the London market; in one sense the parish of Mortlake had a sweeter savour some years since than at present, for there were large fields of lavender, of which but little is now grown.

View of TWICKENHAM, in Middlesex.

View of ISLEWORTH, in Middlesex.

Plate 10. *Engravings from the* New and Complete British Traveller *written by George Augustus Walpole and published by Alex Hogg, 'Kings Arms', No. 16 Paternoster Row on 22 May 1784. The age and condition of the book limits any imaging to an archive photocopier and the quality of the illustrations is impaired.*

A square-rigged Western barge with a crew of five is well illustrated in the view of Twickenham. The unusually large awning may be protecting a perishable cargo from any inclement weather.

Isleworth in c.1780 includes a gang of six halers towing a barge upstream and demonstrates the method of attaching the tow rope to the mast. COURTESY OF THE UNIVERSITY LIBRARY, CAMBRIDGE

Industry was of secondary importance to agriculture in Mortlake's history and of the manufacturing enterprises only one, the brewery, has survived to the present day. A sugar refinery was operated by William Mucklow & Partners before 1688 and the date of its demise is not known, but the premises were acquired by John Sanders in the early 1740s and converted to a pottery. A tapestry works was founded in 1619 under the patronage of Charles I but wound up before the end of that century. A hundred years of ceramics, manufactured initially by John Sanders and later by Joseph Kishere, terminated in the mid-1800s. The only enterprise still operational after a span of two hundred years is the Stag brewery which was and remains the most important industrial activity in Mortlake. It is reported that a brewery existed in the late fifteenth century between the village green and the river, close to its present site. According to the Survey of 1811 (Appendix 2) the brewery occupied land owned by James Weatherstone which he leased to the brewers, John Cartwright Halford and Thomas Weatherstone. These two partners also owned or rented ancillary storehouses, stables and land. A spin-off from the brewery may well have been the profusion of inns and alehouses in Mortlake, no less than eight serving a male population of only eight hundred and of which male infants probably accounted for 50%. John Halford and Thomas Weatherstone jointly owned the Two Brewers alehouse, leased to Sarah Moss, and in his sole name Halford owned the Bull Inn, leased to James Moore. The presence of the brewery gave rise to another trade, that of maltster, and four are identified in the Survey including Thomas Weatherstone who was both a maltster and a brewer, and John Gray, with two malthouses, one 'next river'. Plate 2 (*The Panorama of the Thames*) illustrates a malthouse to the left of Sanders' pottery situated on the river bank. Was this John Gray's malthouse 'next river'? Although malting was another transient industry in Mortlake, its former existence is a pertinent reminder of the importance of the Thames as a commercial artery in the eighteenth and nineteenth centuries. Malt production prospered in the towns and villages of the upper Thames, Berkshire and adjoining counties supplying quality barley, an essential ingredient for brewing beer, the staple drink of country people.

The Western barge was the principal form of water transport operating inland to the west of London Bridge. There was no standardised design for this type of barge – some had a rounded bow, others a swim-headed (punt-like) bow – but there were common features including square undercut sterns and long shallow rudders giving reasonable steerage at slow speeds and reducing to a minimum the risk of grounding on the riverbed. Exceptionally, some of the largest eighteenth century barges were said to be capable of carrying up to two hundred tons of cargo and when fully laden had a draught of only four feet due to their great length and flat bottomed hull. Masts had to be strong enough to withstand the strain of sail or towing and be retractable for shooting bridges. Journeys up and down the river and canals occupied days, not hours, and bargemen's sleeping quarters were provided by a simple awning at the stern of the barge and a straw mattress.

For much of the eighteenth and nineteenth centuries a team of five or six halers was used to tow the barges upstream (Plate 10). Each had a leather breast-strap with a small harness rope which could be attached to a tow-rope fastened to the top of the mast keeping the rope clear of the water and any obstructions. Gradually the use of manpower for towing gave way to horse power. There is no doubt that the river was the prime channel for the transportation of raw materials to the Mortlake potters which could have included sand from the Isle of Wight, clay from Wareham or Poole and coal from the north-east of England. Sea-going barges, known as hoys, were flat-bottomed, swim-headed craft, similar to Western barges but of massive construction, built to sail in rough waters and to beach on shingle or sand wharfs when loading or discharging cargo (Plate 11). Mast and sails were designed to be lowered swiftly and easily for negotiating low bridges and, in order to reduce drift from a cross wind when under sail, leeboards were brought into use. They were fan-shaped wooden constructions, attached by a pivot to each side of a flat-bottomed vessel, which could be lowered into the sea on the side away from the wind in order to diminish leeway. Accommodation was at best a small cabin in

Plate 11. *Tollhouse, Fulham Bridge c.1868. A seagoing hoy beached adjacent to the Fulham tollhouse on the downstream side of Fulham bridge. A fan-shaped leeboard can be seen on the starboard side of the vessel, slightly forward of amidships. The barge would be capable of shipping potter's raw materials, clay from Dorset, sand from the Isle of Wight and coal or wood fuel, for use in the Fulham pottery, completing the short distance from the barge to the potworks by horse and cart.* COURTESY OF THE HAMMERSMITH AND FULHAM ARCHIVES

the stern or an awning similar to the Western barges.

Their cargoes were discharged in the Pool of London between London Bridge and the Tower and transported to Thames-side quays by lighters and then by horse-drawn carts to warehouses or storage depots. The old London Bridge, which survived until 1834, created a partial barrier between sea-going vessels and river barges. Queenshithe dock, situated upstream of London Bridge, was one example of an important depot for receiving bulk supplies from the Pool of London and trans-shipping goods and raw materials to merchants and manufacturers. It is doubtful whether a purpose-built wharf existed in Mortlake in 1745, by which time the brewery was well established and John Sanders had opened his pottery. In all probability flat-bottomed river barges would ground, bows first, on a sloping hard of compacted gravel or sand. The cargo would be manually unloaded to the beach via a gang-plank and carried away by horse and cart. In later years stone or timber quays provided moorings for vessels and derricks or cranes facilitated the discharge of coal, sacks of barley, barrels and other cargoes.

It is not easy to explain why John Sanders, an established Lambeth potter, was persuaded to found a second factory in Mortlake. The two obvious advantages, proximity to a navigable river and the presence of a nearby major market, are equally applicable to other, more favourable sites adjacent to the Thames which are known to have supported potteries. It may well be that William Sanders was residing in Mortlake while working with his father, John Sanders, in Lambeth. The first available rate book shows that William was living in Mortlake in 1754 and it is not improbable that he was a resident in 1745, if not earlier. He married a Mortlake girl in the Parish Church of St. Mary the Virgin and the records read 'William Sanders, bachelor and Sarah …?, spinster of Mortlake Parish, married by licence October 25th 1748'. This connection with Mortlake helps to support the premise that he was probably living in the village before 1745 and therefore knew that the sugarhouse was available and could be converted to a pottery. Dr. David Redstone[7] adds to the picture when he suggests that 'John Sanders, presumably looking for a potential pottery site for his son William, found a disused sugar house by the river Thames at Mortlake and insured it for £700 with the Hand-in-Hand insurance company in December 1745'.

In addition to his Lambeth enterprise John Sanders now had a Mortlake pothouse with his son William as the potential 'managing director' and it only required raw materials together with a modest workforce to commence production. It appears probable that Mortlake was chosen for the new venture partly because William's residence happened to be in close proximity to the disused sugar refinery and in the early days of the Industrial Revolution it was not unusual for the 'master' to live on or near the works. Potters were surprisingly mobile in the eighteenth century and the nucleus of a workforce may have been recruited from experienced personnel at Sanders' Lambeth pottery. At a later date, and in the same context, there can be little doubt that when Benjamin Kishere (1)★ was appointed manager or supervisor at Mortlake he moved from Lambeth, ultimately leading to the inception of Joseph Kishere's pottery.

One further consideration may have been relevant in choosing Mortlake for Sanders' potworks. Whilst the Thames was the key to the successful distribution of raw materials

Plate 12. *An undated drawing of a 'View of Kew from the North' including Kew Bridge which opened for traffic on 4 June 1759. It consisted of eleven arches, the two piers and their dependent arches at each side being built of brick and stone, while the seven intermediate arches were constructed entirely of wood. It was replaced by a new stone bridge in 1789.* COURTESY OF THE HAMMERSMITH AND FULHAM ARCHIVES

and merchandise to the east and west of London, it was also a natural barrier to the movement of goods across the river. Until Westminster Bridge opened in 1750, the single bridge serving the capital was London Bridge which successfully handled a continuous flow of heavily laden, horse-drawn carts and wagons for over six hundred years until its replacement in 1830. In 1745 only one bridge existed between London and Teddington and it happened to be the old Putney Bridge, no more than three miles from Mortlake. Around this date a crossing was proposed at Kew although the bridge was not completed until 1759 (Plate 12). In appraising the viability of a manufacturing site any entrepreneur would have due regard to the adequacy of the transport network, both existing and proposed, and we can assume that John Sanders would be no exception.

Rocque's 1746 index maps, showing Kew Bridge and Westminster Bridge in existence, are somewhat misleading. However, the larger scale versions of the same maps describe Kew Bridge as 'proposed' and it is also reasonable to assume that Westminster Bridge, in its planning stage in 1738, was under construction by 1746.

~ Chapter Two ~

THE KISHERE POTTERY

The origin of the Kishere pottery is inextricably interwoven with John Sanders, the Lambeth potter, who established his pottery in Mortlake over fifty years before Joseph Kishere (8) built his first kiln. It is in Lambeth that we begin the search for the Kishere family roots and the connection with John Sanders.

The records of the Hand-in-Hand Insurance Company in the Guildhall Library have been thoroughly researched by Frank Britton and are extensively quoted in his book describing the London Delftware potteries.[1] From this source we gather that by 1743 John Sanders had established a delftware pottery in Glasshouse Street, Lambeth. The year can be predated to 1742 when 'John Bates, son of Henry Bates, [was apprenticed] to John Sanders of Lambeth, Potter. Consideration £10/10/-'.[2] Subsequent improvements to

Plate 13. *A view of the River Thames at low tide 'Near Vauxhall Bridge'. Drawn and engraved by F.V. Martens. Lithograph on paper 1829. By 1753 John Sanders and his partner Nicholas Crisp had purchased a windmill in Nine Elms which is described in the records of the Hand-in-Hand Insurance Company as '4 sto. High 32ft. dia with a stage round do 9ft. wide', situated 'on the NW side of the Road from Vauxhall to Nine Elms'.[1] It was built on the Thames bank, at the water's edge, by the mouth of a creek. Appendix 6 traces its history from 1753 to 1843.*

the pottery included a new kiln which was operational by 1751 and in the same year Sanders was joined by Nicholas Crisp, described as a jeweller. The partners made two further investments, firstly acquiring the right to mine Cornish soapstone and secondly purchasing a windmill in Nine Elms capable of grinding potters' raw materials (Plate 13). A new kiln, together with the sourcing and facilities for processing soapstone, indicate an intention to manufacture porcelain in addition to delftware, or at least to experiment with the new body. Capital would have been required to finance these initiatives which may help to explain the introduction of a jeweller, Nicholas Crisp, as the new partner. In the years 1745 to 1751 factories in Bristol, Derby, Worcester, Longton Hall and, within London, Chelsea and Bow were producing soft-paste porcelain, some containing soapstone, and it is not improbable that John Sanders decided to compete with these firms although the degree of commercial success is doubtful.

The first consignment of soapstone was delivered in late 1752, some fifteen months after engrossing the mining agreement. Trial firings, or perhaps full scale production, commenced soon afterwards but an announcement in *The Public Advertiser* of 21 May 1753[3] implies a failure to achieve the desired quality in the initial batches. It reads:

> At Mr Sander's near the Plate Glasshouse, Vauxhall is now to be sold, a strong and useful Manufacture of Porcelaine Ware made there of English Materials. The Degree of Success, which has already attended the several attempts, lately made in England for establishing a Manufactory of Porcelaine in Imitation of the Ware of China, gives Reason to hope, that this Design will still continue to be carried on, till it arrive at its due Degree of Perfection.

Archaeological excavations at the pottery site in 1980 and 1987 produced wasters resulting in the recognition of some Sanders wares which had previously remained unidentified. John Sanders died in 1758 and the production of porcelain is unlikely to have continued much beyond 1760 when the original soapstone licence was transferred to John Baddeley and William Yates, Staffordshire potters. An alternative source of raw materials could have been substituted or existing stocks may have supported limited production, but a further crisis in 1763 almost certainly brought an end to this porcelain venture. In that year Nicholas Crisp was declared bankrupt and on 31 May and 1 June 1764 the Assignees arranged an auction of:

> All the entire Stock of their valuable Porcelain Manufactory at Lambeth consisting of curious Figures, all sorts of ornamental Toys, Knife-Handles, and Variety of all Kinds of useful Sorts, etc.

In 1766, or possibly earlier, Nicholas Crisp moved to Bovey Tracey where he either established or took over an existing pottery[4] in order to continue his experiments into the production of true porcelain. Before his death in 1774 Crisp may have achieved his objective but, if so, he probably plagiarised the successful recipes and techniques developed by Cookworthy.

In addition to the Lambeth pothouse John Sanders decided to expand the production of delftware by establishing a second pottery in Mortlake. It is known that a sugarhouse (refinery?) existed between the Thames and the High Street in 1688 or earlier[5] and, as already mentioned, these premises were acquired by John Sanders. After conversion the site consisted of a dwelling house, a five storey pothouse, stables and lofts, two warehouses and a mill house. By 1744 or 1745 the pottery was in production.

Anderson's statement[6] that William Sanders established 'the first pottery for delftware in Mortlake between 1742 and 1752' appears to contradict the Hand-in-Hand fire policy records. They show John Sanders as the insured party in 1745 and his son William in 1752, implying that John, not William, founded the Sanders Mortlake potworks. On this evidence we can accept that John Sanders financed the purchase of the site. However, William, born in 1702 or 1703, would have been in his early forties when the factory opened and, if he was brought up to the pottery business with a working knowledge of delftware production, there is every reason to believe that he was competent to manage his father's new venture from its inception. In those days insurance cover was usually written for a period of seven years and in 1752 William, as 'managing director' and occupier of the premises, may well have renewed the insurance on behalf of his father or on his own behalf if he had a legal interest in the property by that date. In the early years an owner and manager relationship between John and William perhaps helps to reconcile Anderson's statement with the Hand-in-Hand records.

At this point it is apposite to reintroduce the name of Benjamin Kishere (1). As mentioned earlier, the story begins in Lambeth where there is confirmation of a family connection. Frank Britton[1] lists two Lambeth potters, Edward Kishere (1719–38) and John Kishere (1724–63), and the Apprentice records[2] also include a reference to an Edward Kishere: '1719 Kishere Charles son of Edward Kishere of Lambeth Potter to Sam Wheeler Citizen and Tallow Chandler'.

The most interesting discovery, however, is to be found in the Lambeth Archives Collection containing the baptism records for St. Mary Church, Lambeth with an entry on 27 June 1731 reading 'Benjamin, son of Samuel Kishere and Mary his wife'. Was this Benjamin the future patriarch of the Mortlake Kisheres? Positive proof is lacking but there are a number of pointers towards an affirmative answer. It may or may not be a major clue but Benjamin's first child, Samuel (3), who died in infancy, could have been named after his grandfather. Prior to 1759, the year of Benjamin's marriage, there is no mention of the Kishere name in the Mortlake Parish Records suggesting that he was born and spent his formative years outside the parish of Mortlake. Other relevant facts include:

- John Sanders established his Lambeth pottery in 1742 or 1743
- John Sanders' daughter, Hannah, was also christened in St. Mary Church, Lambeth on 7 August 1730
- Anderson states that Benjamin was one of the leading hands in Sanders' pottery in 1759
- The earliest Poor Rate Book confirming Benjamin's residence in Mortlake is dated July 1760
- The misspelling of Kershaw for Kishere in that entry, together with the absence of a first name, suggests an unfamiliarity with a newcomer to the village

Using these facts it is tempting to reconstruct, at least in theory, Benjamin Kishere's life

Plate 14. *An etching on paper drawn and engraved by Thomas Priest c.1742, described as 'A view of Mortlake with figures drawing in fishing nets'. Depending upon the accuracy of the drawing, one of the tall buildings to the right of the church tower may be, or may represent, the sugarhouse which existed in 1742 and shortly after that date was purchased by John Sanders for conversion to a pottery. The insurance records make reference to a five storey potworks amongst other ancillary buildings. Another interesting detail is seen on the river bank, just left of centre, where a sign may well be welcoming the river folk to the Queen's Head alehouse.*

COURTESY OF THE GUILDHALL LIBRARY, CORPORATION OF LONDON

story. Born in 1731 he was brought up in Lambeth by his parents, Samuel and Mary Kishere, and on leaving school in 1743 at the age of twelve he probably worked for John Sanders at his Lambeth pottery, learning the art of manufacturing delftware. In the 1740s there were other delftware factories in the vicinity of Lambeth and the assumption that Benjamin was employed by John Sanders hinges to some extent on the knowledge that the Sanders and Kishere families attended the same church and would know each other.

John Sanders died in 1758, leaving the Lambeth business jointly to his son William and his son-in-law Henry Richards. However, there are no references to Henry Richards (not even an '& Co') in the Mortlake rate books or the fire insurance policies and it appears likely that the Mortlake copyhold and business, if not already in William's possession, was bequeathed exclusively to him. With his additional responsibilities stemming from the shared management of Lambeth, William may have decided that an experienced and reliable supervisor was needed at Mortlake. While Benjamin Kishere was in the employ of John Sanders in Lambeth he would probably be known to William and the likelihood becomes a certainty in 1758 following William's direct involvement in that business. Using Anderson's date of 1759 we can surmise that William persuaded Benjamin Kishere to move from Lambeth to Mortlake where he rented a house and was appointed foreman of the pottery.

By this date Benjamin Kishere was twenty-eight years old. He married Susanna (2) on 23 June 1759 in the Mortlake Parish Church of St. Mary and their first child Samuel was christened there some twelve months later. Having established Benjamin as a resident of Mortlake, and acknowledging that part of his early history is conjectural, although plausible, this is now an opportune time to complete the account of Sanders' pottery.

As already recorded, **John Sanders** established the Mortlake works in 1744 or 1745 and on his death in 1758 the copyhold was bequeathed to his son, **William Sanders,** who continued the production of delftware. In 1784 William died and the copyhold passed to his son, John Sanders, aged twenty-five, who was soon joined by a partner, then trading as **Sanders & Vernon** or John Sanders & Co.; the latter style is recorded in the Poor Rate Book for March 1786. This new partner was probably John Vernon, since the name appears regularly in the Poor Rate Books between 1772 and 1798.

In all probability John Sanders did not share his father and grandfather's enthusiasm for the business of manufacturing ceramics. Entering into a partnership with Vernon is one indication of his indifference and the following notice dated 1 April 1789 in the *Daily Advertiser* demonstrates his intention to sell the copyhold of the pottery site:

Sale of a Copyhold Estate, comprising four Brick Tenements, with a Millhouse, Stable, and large Garden on the Banks of the Thames, in the Occupation of Mess. Sanders & Co. Tenants at Will; 'the Premises are remarkably eligible to be converted into a Malthouse, or for the Coal and Timber Trade,' Enquiries (inter alia) to John Cooks, Mortlake, or at the Premises.

Plate 15. *A drawing of the Fulham pottery in the 1860s, graphically illustrating the construction of a kiln inside a kilnhouse with the chimney section protruding through the roof. Such buildings usually had workshops on the upper floors and no doubt Sanders' bottle oven, as shown in Leigh's* Panorama of the Thames, *would have closely resembled the Fulham examples. From Watford's* Old and New London *Vol. 6, 1888-1893.*

Plate 16. *Goblet with applied emblem and motto of the Beefsteak Club. Probably **Kishere** factory c.1800. H. 8½in. (21.6cm).*   COURTESY OF THE BRIGHTON MUSEUM & ART GALLERY – WILLETT 595/328609

The details tally closely with those written in the Hand-in-Hand fire policy of 1745. A sale did not materialise and another five years passed before John Sanders achieved his objective by becoming a landlord of the site and no longer a potter.

In 1794 the Sanders & Vernon partnership terminated and John Sanders, whilst retaining the copyhold as evidenced by the Survey of 1811 (Appendix 2), leased the pottery to a succession of potters. **Thomas Norris** occupied the site from 1794 to 1801 and his name appears as one of ten signatories to a price fixing agreement executed in 1795, all the participants being 'manufacturers of brown stoneware in the vicinity of London.'[7] With the decline in popularity of delftware in the closing years of the nineteenth century, Thomas Norris probably added stoneware to the pottery's output and Anderson believed 'there were two kilns, one for white ware and the other for coarser work'.

Pressick Dodd had taken over the business by April 1802 according to the rate books. He is assumed to have been a financier and if so would have required the support of an experienced potter. This may have been the role of a Mr. Gurney whose name is associated with Sanders' factory and who was almost certainly related to George and John B. Gurney, Lambeth potters in the 1780s. Anderson states that 'Gurney lived in the High Street and had a good position in the works'. There is a further reference to this gentleman in 'Mortlake Memories' which appears to be a regular contribution to the *Richmond and Twickenham Times* written by John Eustace Anderson. An extract from his article at an unrecorded date in 1914 reads 'About ninety years ago a Mr. Gurney carried on a pottery where St. Mary's Wharf is at the present time, and employed about six hands'. At a much later date, 26 July 1974, the same newspaper names Gurney & Dodd as the joint proprietors of the business in 1804. It has to be admitted that newspaper articles are notoriously unreliable and if a partnership ever existed it was of short duration and would have been dissolved in 1804.

The business then came into the hands of **William Wagstaff** who was actively manufacturing delft and stoneware at Vauxhall from 1793 to 1802. He was also a subscriber to the 1795 price fixing agreement mentioned above and, by 1804, had taken over from Pressick Dodd in Mortlake. The dates are taken from the Hand-in-Hand policy records (fire cover on the Vauxhall site lapsed in 1802) and his inclusion in the 1804 Mortlake rate books helps to confirm that William Wagstaff left Vauxhall and after a gap of two years recommenced production of delft and stoneware at Sanders' pottery.

One further change of occupancy is recorded. **John Wisker** inherited the enterprise following the death of his uncle William Wagstaff in 1809 and the Survey of 1811 (Appendix 2) confirms his tenancy of a house, pottery and yard valued at £112; the copyhold was still held by John Sanders. Fourteen years later the history of Sanders' pottery turns full circle. In 1823 John Wisker transferred production of delftware from Mortlake to Glasshouse Street, Lambeth, which was the pottery established by the original John Sanders in c.1742. The Mortlake site may have remained unoccupied for some years, being described as 'empty' in the manorial court rolls of 1829, and at some date after 1830 the premises were converted to a malthouse. This may well have been an extension of the existing malthouse, abutting Sanders' pottery, as illustrated in Leigh's *Panorama of the Thames* c.1825. According to Charles Hailstone, the property 'was later described as a range of malthouses' which suggests that the two sites were incorporated into an enlarged malthouse.

Returning to the Kishere story, Benjamin's youngest son Joseph (8), born 1768, worked at Sanders' Mortlake pottery. If his employment began immediately after leaving school, in say 1780, he would have been apprenticed initially to William Sanders and subsequently to Sanders & Vernon, a 'turn over' proudly recorded on Joseph Kishere's trade card – 'Late Apprentice to Messrs. Sanders & Vernon, Potters' – which is dated to the late eighteenth century when Joseph was managing his own business. In his late twenties or early thirties he had the confidence, expertise and capital to build a potworks for the manufacture of salt-glazed stoneware. Anderson provides two clues in dating the commissioning of the pottery when he tells us firstly that Joseph's bride brought 'a little

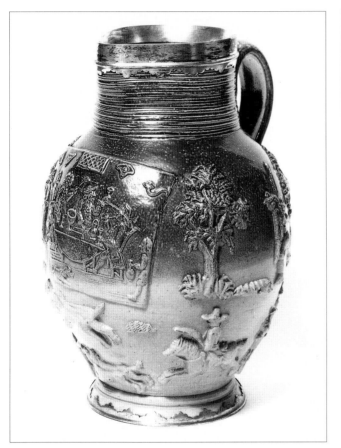

Plate 17. *Hunting jug, with the 'Punch Party'. Rim engraved 'Staffordshire 7th Dec. 1786'. Probably **Sanders** factory. H. 8¼in. (21cm).* COURTESY OF THE NATIONAL MUSEUM AND GALLERY ON MERSEYSIDE,1966.89

Plate 18. *Hunting jug with the 'Cupids' Procession' and profile heads of George III and Queen Caroline, perhaps commemorating the restoration of the King's health in 1789. Probably **Sanders** factory. Height and owner unknown.*

money' to the marriage, and secondly that a prize in the state lottery shared with his brother Benjamin (4) 'gave him a start in life'. The lottery winnings are of little help but Joseph's marriage to Ann Griffin (9) is known to have been solemnised on 26 April 1795 and, turning to the rate books, there is an initial entry in September 1795 for Joseph Kishere, rental £12. Further entries occur under a general heading of East Sheen Lane. In the Poor Rate Book of September 1797, however, the property is annotated 'Emp' [Empty] and Joseph Kishere and family had moved to the High Street. Two months later, November 1797, the *rate collector* added 'Paid for potters' after Joseph's name in the East Sheen Lane section of the Surveyors' Rate Book and, presumably, temporary accommodation had been found for one or two employees in his former house. On this evidence there can be little doubt that the Kishere pottery was in production in 1797, some two years after his marriage to Ann.

The Kishere enterprise was a modest operation from the outset and by 1811 the business premises were valued at only £30 compared with Sanders' pottery valued at £112. Using the available references it is possible to recreate a picture of the site which

Plate 19. *Two images of a documentary mug with impressed date of 1830 and marked* **'Kishere Moatlake'.** *Decorated with applied coat of arms and dedicated to R.P. Alvin. For detailed description see page 42. H. 6½in. (16.5cm).*

Plate 20. *The base of the mug illustrated in Plate 19 showing the impressed mark* **'Kishere Moatlake'.** *Moatlake is thought to be a colloquialism, echoing the pronunciation of Mortlake by some of the rustic residents.*

Plate 21. *Chamber pot. An abundance of sprigs decorate the outside of the bowl and extend to the inside base. Marked (twice)* **'Kishere Pottery Mortlake Surry'** *and 'T Humfrey 1842'. H. 5⅞in. (15cm).* Courtesy of the Museum of London 98/39

Plate 22. *Lifelike images of a thrower, using a kick-wheel, and his 'ball maker' assistant, usually a young boy, responsible for 'wedging' the clay. Both figures were modelled and produced in the late 19th century by the four Martin brothers who manufactured salt-glazed stoneware in London and Southall between 1873 and 1912.* Courtesy of the Trustees of the Victoria & Albert Museum

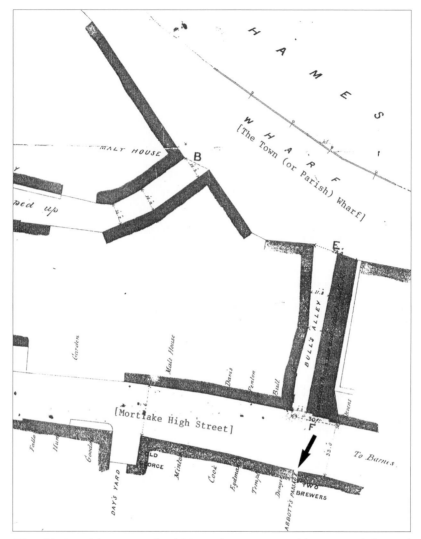

Plate 23. *Detail from a map dated 13 March 1865 prepared for Messrs. Phillips and Wigan (Mortlake Brewery) proposing the enclosure of Thames Street within the brewery and the widening of the High Street and Bull's Alley in compensation. It shows Abbott's Passage (arrowed), identifying the former site of Joseph Kishere's pottery directly opposite Bull's Alley. Abbott's Passage, adjacent to the Two Brewers public house, was created when the site was redeveloped in the mid-1800s.*

was situated on the south side of the High Street and to the west of Mortlake church. It had a width of about 35 feet (10.5 metres) and a depth of approximately 115 feet (35 metres) extending from the High Street to Vineyard Path (known as Back Lane prior to 1896), an irregular alleyway lying to the south and following the general line of the High Street. A dwelling house fronted on to the High Street with access to a yard, presumably gravelled or cobbled, accommodating stables and a shed. The site was immediately opposite Bulls Alley which led directly to the River Thames and, most importantly, to the town (or parish) wharf facilitating the transportation of fuel and raw materials (Plate

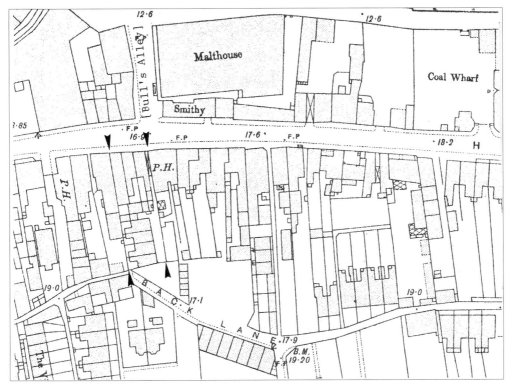

Plate 24. *By orientating the 'brewery map' (Plate 38) with this detail from a later map of 1894-96 the Kishere pottery is readily located. The redevelopment carried out by Thomas Abbott is clearly shown, i.e. three terraced properties fronting the High Street and four terraced cottages in Martha Place at the rear together with a narrow access passage to the High Street named Abbott's Passage.*

23). The pottery itself abutted the Vineyard Path and its kiln, if fired only once each week, must have discharged an obnoxious cocktail of gases and acids on the unfortunate local residents. We have to assume that ancillary buildings and sheds were built near or around the kiln. The survey of 1811 (Appendix 2) lists a second site consisting of a tenement and warehouse, valued at £6, which could have been used for storing raw materials and/or finished goods. Both sites, the pottery and the warehouse, were owned by a David Seal and let or leased to Joseph Kishere.

Charles Hailstone mentions that the land (the copyhold of the pottery site) was sold to Benjamin Kishere (4) in 1819, although no reference is made to the warehouse site. The emergence of Joseph's elder brother Benjamin as the new 'freeholder' and landlord is somewhat unexpected unless Joseph, who was far more involved with the site, did not have the cash resources available to finance the purchase. Joseph continued to work the pottery and must have been granted a tenancy or new lease by his brother. These events give further credence to the date of 1797 for Joseph's move from East Sheen Lane to the High Street. If he was initially granted a twenty-one year lease it would have expired in 1818 and David Seal, the landlord, or his successors in title, may have decided to sell the copyhold rather than enter into a new rental agreement.

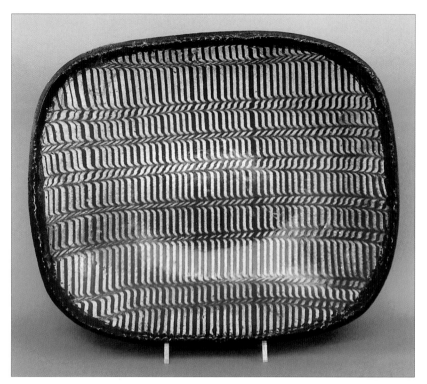

Plate 25. Slipware dish, impressed 'Abbott Potter' (illustrated) c.1843-5. Width 16¼in. (42.5cm). COURTESY OF THE TRUSTEES OF THE VICTORIA & ALBERT MUSEUM

Plate 26. Hunting jug, with the 'Punch Party' plaque. Probably **Sanders** *factory, about 1780-1790. H. 9¾in. (24.8cm).*
COURTESY OF THE TRUSTEES OF THE VICTORIA & ALBERT MUSEUM
(C.64-1981)

Plate 27. Hunting jug with Type II windmill and Toby Philpot. Impressed on the face of the jug 'T & E BOYS 1820'. **Kishere** *factory. H. 7¼in. (18.5cm).*

COURTESY OF THE MUSEUM OF LONDON, C66

Plate 28. Quart and pint beer mugs, with 'Punch Party' and 'Drunken Boors'. Probably **Kishere** factory, the pint mug with mount hallmarked 1798. H. 6⅞in. (17.5cm) and 5⅛in. (13cm). PRIVATE COLLECTION

Plate 29. Hunting jug, with plaque of the 'Cupids' Procession'. **Sanders** or **Kishere** factory, about 1790-1800. H. 6¾in. (17.3cm).
COURTESY OF THE TRUSTEES OF THE VICTORIA & ALBERT MUSEUM, C.66–1981

Plate 30. An unmarked, baluster style, hunting jug with silver mounts hallmarked 1799. Decorated with a plaque of the 'Punch Party', tree, hounds etc. Probably **Kishere** factory. H. 9⅜in. (24cm).
PRIVATE COLLECTION

Other ceramic historians make reference to Sir Richard Phillips' account of his walk to Kew in 1817[8] when he visited a High Street 'manufactory of Delft and stoneware, for which among potters Mortlake was then famous'. This pottery employed 'a dozen workmen at 20s. a week'. Anderson is convinced that he is describing Kishere's works whereas Robin Hildyard ascribes Sir Richard's comments to Sanders' pottery which was then in the hands of John Wisker. This attribution has to be the preferred alternative in that Joseph Kishere's Pottery has never been positively linked with the production of delftware and he is unlikely ever to have employed as many as a dozen workmen. In fact there is every reason to believe that his was basically a family business using some hired labour, particularly in the early years when his children were too young to take an active role in the pottery.

At a later date, however, his children did become involved, Anderson stating that Joseph's two sons, William (26) and John Griffin (33), were both brought up to the pottery business and his daughter Susan (29) sometimes helped 'to stamp out the hunting figures in clay and place them on the jugs'. William, born 1800, almost certainly made a career of potting and after leaving school in c.1814 probably worked alongside his father. John Griffin, born 1816, was sixteen years younger than his brother and he may not have shared William's commitment to the manufacture of brown stoneware. His working life was mainly connected with horse-drawn transport; he described himself firstly as a carter in the June 1841 Census Return, when he was twenty-five years of age, and then as a brewer at the time of his marriage a few months later. The death of his parents in 1834, when John was in his late teens, possibly triggered his departure from the family business which was inherited by William.

There are three examples of Joseph Kishere supplying taverns and inns with drinking utensils. In addition to the trade card (Plate 47), two half-gallon jars recorded in John Anderson's Stoneware Collection (Appendix 8) were respectively impressed with the names of the Prince Blucher, Twickenham and the White Hart Inn, Barnes. Does this suggest the principal commercial niche in which Joseph Kishere chose to operate? By selling direct to the consumer, cutting out the middleman and trading from a low cost base, he would be favourably placed to undersell his competitors. There is one other pointer to this business philosophy. Sanders' pottery produced similar wares, not marked with the manufacturer's name, suggesting that their output was planned for the London and provincial china dealers who were zealous in concealing from customers the source of supply in order to retain their loyalty and preserve the retailer's profit margin. In contrast Joseph Kishere was forthright in marking much of his output with the name and address of his pottery and encouraging direct sales. The Staffordshire potters were very alive to the importance and power of the chinamen and for many years there were few transgressors of this unwritten code of practice.

The presence of two brown stoneware exhibits in the collection of the Brighton Museum and Art Gallery indicates Joseph Kishere's willingness to accept special commissions. A goblet (Plate 16) attributed to Kishere dated c.1800 and bearing the emblem of The Beefsteak Club, a gridiron, and motto reading 'Beef and Liberty', must have been a special order. The forerunner of the present club was founded in 1735 by the harlequin, Henry Rich, and George Lambert, a landscape painter. They strictly

*Plate 31. Jug, with profile bust of Nelson. Probably **Mortlake**, about 1805. H. 7¾in. (19.5cm).*   NOEL HUME COLLECTION (CHIPSTONE FOUNDATION)

limited the membership to twenty-four (men only) drawn from the aristocracy and the arts. Even the Prince of Wales, who became Prince Regent (1810) and later King George IV (1820-1830), was obliged to wait until a vacancy occurred. Lunch, provided every Saturday between November and June, included beefsteaks, followed by toasted cheese and washed down with port, porter, punch and whisky toddy. The members wore a uniform of blue coats and buff waistcoats with buttons bearing the gridiron emblem. From their first meeting room in the Covent Garden Theatre, the club subsequently moved to a number of coffee houses and taverns, and finally the Lyceum. When the Covent Garden Theatre burned down the original gridiron, recovered from the ashes, was used as decoration in the meeting rooms and became the Society's emblem.

By 1867 support for the Beefsteak Club had gradually waned and it was dissolved in that year. However, the name and emblem were adopted by a newly formed dining club which opened in 1876 and still flourishes in premises acquired towards the end of the nineteenth century in Irving Street, off Leicester Square. The membership list, substantially increased from twenty-four (but still all men), has included Rudyard Kipling, Harold Macmillan, Malcolm Sargent, Osbert Lancaster and John Betjeman.

Plate 32. *Hunting jug, with plaque of the 'Punch Party'. Marked 'J★K' impressed (illustrated).* **Kishere** *factory, c.1800. H.8⅝in. (22cm).*

Plate 33. *Hunting jug, with oval plaque of 'Race Horses' and post windmill. Probably* **Kishere** *factory, about 1810. H. 7in. (17.8cm).*

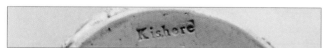

Plate 34. *Hunting jug, with post windmill. Marked* **'Kishere'** *(illustrated), about 1810-20. H. 8½in. (21.8cm).*

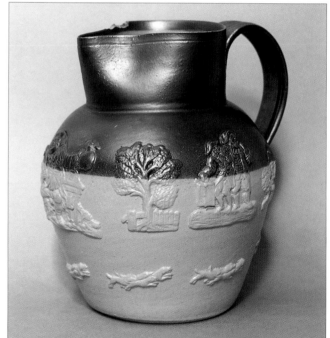

Plate 35. *Hunting jug, with Toby Philpot. Marked* **'KISHERE POTTERY MORTLAKE SURRY'** *(illustrated), about 1830-40. H. 7¾in. (20cm).*

~ 44 ~

Plate 36. *Loving cup, with 'Drunken Boors' and 'Punch Party'.* **Kishere** *factory, about 1800. H. 8in. (20.4cm).*

PRIVATE COLLECTION

Plate 37. *Tobacco pots, with plaques of 'Drunken Boors' and 'Toby Philpot'. Both marked* **'KISHERE MOATLAKE'** *(sic). About 1810-20. Max H. 5¼in. (13.4cm).*

LEFT, COURTESY OF THE TRUSTEES OF THE VICTORIA & ALBERT MUSEUM
RIGHT, PRIVATE COLLECTION

A second exhibit in the Brighton Museum and Art Gallery is a specially commissioned, commemorative mug with the mark 'Kishere Moatlake' impressed in the base (Plates 19 and 20). The body is decorated with an applied medallion carrying a shield, a chevron, three barrels and a motto 'In God is all our Trust'. Beneath the medallion a date, 1830, and a name, R.P. Alvin, have been impressed into the clay. Further decoration is provided by an abundance of vine leaves and grapes surrounding the medallion and even extending to the strap handle. The Museum's records ascribe the mug to the Brewers' Society (formed in 1822) by which name The Country Brewers' Society was generally known. Unfortunately the minutes of the Society for 1830 make no reference to R.P. Alvin and he did not attend the AGM or any of the meetings in that year. The College of Arms states that the arms on the mug 'were granted to The Worshipful Company of Vintners of the City of London on 17 September 1447. They are blazoned: Sable a Chevron between three Wine Tuns Argent'. However, this gives rise to other problems – the Latin motto of the Vintners' Company has been substituted by 'In God is all our Trust' which happens to be the motto of The Worshipful Company of Brewers and, in addition, the Brewers' archivist is unable to find any trace of R.P. Alvin. Perhaps the unusual combination of arms and motto was the adopted emblem of The Country Brewers' Society and, despite the absence of any proof, the mug must have been commissioned and presented to R.P. Alvin in recognition of services to a livery company or trade association or a commercial organisation. He was a resident of Mortlake in 1826 and earlier but the Poor Rate Book of October 1832, the next available reference point, describes him as 'late R.P. Alvin'.

A marked and dated exhibit in the Museum of London, a chamber pot (Plate 21) is decorated on the outside of the bowl with a plethora of sprigs; a tree and fence, watchman and drunkard, a group of two seated drinkers and a single seated drinker, a windmill, and mounted huntsmen and hounds. A sense of humour must have persuaded the potter to continue the sprigging to the inside base of the pot with a single seated drinker, a mounted huntsman and hounds. The impressed mark 'Kishere Pottery Mortlake Surry' appears twice on the base and 'T. Humfrey 1842' is stamped on the surface opposite the handle. This name and date are also found on a colander in a private collection.

Joseph Kishere was not destined to emulate the lasting achievements of a John Doulton. Kishere ran his own business for thirty-six years within the confines of the same site where there was little or no room for expansion. It is assumed that he enjoyed a reasonable standard of living but evidently lacked the ambition – or possibly the capital – to develop the operation. None the less his name, and that of his pottery, has survived to the present day, due in no small measure to the impressed marking of his wares and Anderson's chronicle.

For the next nine years William Kishere owned the works, either as the lessee or as the copyholder if the 'freehold' interest had been acquired at some stage from his uncle Benjamin. The personal grief following the death of his father must have been deepened by the ending of their close working relationship, and the subsequent employment of John Pollard would be a necessary, although sad, replacement. Contemporary directories indicate that William was supplementing his manufacturing profits with insurance

Plate 38. *Small hunting jug, with plaque of 'Drunken Boors'. Probably* **Sanders** *factory, the mount hall-marked 1795.*
COURTESY OF THE SHEFFIELD CITY MUSEUM L.1943.667

Plate 39. *Hunting jug, with oval plaque of 'Race Horses'. Probably* **Kishere** *factory, about 1800-1810. H. 8in. (20.5cm).*
COURTESY OF THE FITZWILLIAM MUSEUM, G1.1209

commission. He is listed in Pigot's Directories of 1838 and 1840 under two headings, firstly as a potter and secondly as a Fire and Life Assurance Agent with the Royal Exchange. There is nothing to suggest that he made any radical changes to the well-established Kishere tradition. William died suddenly in April 1843 and his widow continued to occupy the premises, according to the rate book, until at least October 1844, but we cannot be sure that the pottery remained in production.

By February 1845 the site had been sold to Thomas Abbott, subsequently a Mortlake resident, who granted a tenancy to his brother John Abbott. The latter's name appears in Pigot's Directories for 1826, 1838 and 1840, firstly as a Tallow Chandler, then a Tallow Chandler and China Dealer and thirdly as a China, Glass etc. Dealer, trading from premises in Hill Street, Richmond. It may have been his objective to integrate manufacturing with an established retail outlet and his son Thomas was given the responsibility of running the pottery. Whilst such a concept appeared to have some merit it was an evident failure, lasting for little more than two years and leading to the closure and ultimate demolition of Kishere's pottery after a working life of some fifty years.

Plate 40. *Left. Pint beer mug with Type II windmill and thatchers at work on a cottage. Marked* **'KISHERE'.** *c.1820 H. 5⅝in. (14.4cm). Right. Hunting jug with a sprigged sequence of 'The Meet' – horses at rest, horsemen climbing a fence and hounds at the kill. Marked* **'KISHERE MOATLAKE'** (sic) *c.1810. H. 7in. (17.8cm).* COURTESY OF THE MUSEUM OF LONDON, LEFT A.27231, RIGHT A28220

Possession of the site reverted to the elder Thomas Abbott who maximised its development potential by clearing the plot and building three terraced properties fronting the High Street and four terraced cottages, known as Martha Place, at the rear. The cottages abutted the Vineyard Path and were erected on ground formerly occupied by the defunct pottery. A narrow path called Abbott's Passage was constructed on the eastern flank of the site connecting Martha Place to the High Street (Plate 24).

The last reference to the Kishere site is recorded by Charles Hailstone – 'when the Vineyard site was prepared for back gardens in recent years quantities of broken pottery came to light, including the mark Kishere Pottery Mortlake Surry'.

Chapter Three

PRODUCTION TECHNIQUES

Then, as the workers proceeded round the dome, a weird scene presented itself. The leaping stokers proceeding to the several holes and the walking burners feeding in the salt with their long ladles were seen through an ever denser screen of fumes. Here the whole formed a picture worthy of the pen of a Milton or a Dante, worthy of the pencil of the greatest painter who ever tried to render hell on canvas. We are told in the book of 'Revelation' that the devil was cast into the lake of fire and brimstone and, after seeing this, I can imagine that.

This is J.F. Blacker's[1] graphic description of salting a kiln, an operation to which he was invited in May 1922 at the Lambeth potworks of Doulton. The awesome eruption of fire and smoke results from a chemical reaction within the kiln, a technique used in the production of salt-glazed stoneware and thought to have originated in the Rhineland possibly as early as the fourteenth century. It can be expressed in the shorthand of a chemical equation based on formulae quoted by Frank and Janet Hamer in *The Potters Dictionary of Materials and Techniques*[2] and by Peter Starkey, the author of *Saltglaze:*[3]

$$2NaCl + H_2O \rightarrow Na_2O + 2HCl \rightarrow \text{Discharged as a gas}$$

Salt (Sodium Chloride)   (Water)   (Sodium Oxide)   (Hydrogen Chloride)

$$+$$

$$SiO_2Al_2O_3$$
Clay
(Includes Aluminium Oxide and Silica)

$$=$$

$$Na_2OSiO_2Al2O_3$$
Saltglaze
(Sodium Alumino-Silicate)

The process of salt glazing, however, involves far more than a chemical reaction. As will be seen later, it is a technology based on science but subordinate to the art and skill of the potter coupled with a thorough understanding of the idiosyncrasies of his own kiln with its unique characteristics. It does not require a degree in chemistry to understand the theory of what happens in the kiln, although achieving consistently good results in practice is problematical and it must have been even more difficult in the late eighteenth and early nineteenth centuries. Nevertheless, the potters of those days were successful in producing quality wares and, in the absence of modern firing aids, they relied on the training received during apprenticeship and on practical experience. The first requirement is a minimum kiln temperature of 1100°C at which stage the de-composition of salt (sodium chloride) will commence if water is also present. The addition of a small quantity of water to the salt ensures rapid decomposition and the presence of steam converts the resulting sodium oxide and hydrogen chloride into gases. Vaporised sodium oxide then enters the porous surface of the pots, combining with the silica present in the clay to produce a glaze (sodium alumino-silicate) with the aluminium oxide acting as a catalyst. Dependent upon the composition of the clay, the result varies between a high gloss finish and a mottled surface, frequently referred to as 'orange peel'.

Charles Hailstone[4] reports that an excavation of the Kishere site for conversion to back gardens uncovered pottery shards, but as he makes no reference to the remains or foundations of any structures we shall never know the type, size and design of the kiln in use at the pottery. Both up-draught and down-draught kilns have been used for salt glazing. The bottle-shaped, up-draught kiln was perfected in the Potteries by the late eighteenth century but it had an efficiency of only 5% or, conversely, an enormous 95% heat loss. A more efficient, domed, down-draught kiln had to be the preferred option and a present-day, commercial producer, Errington Reay & Co. Ltd. based in Northumberland, has been using a kiln of this type since their business was founded over 120 years ago. Turning again to Blacker, he is describing a down-draught kiln when he writes:

> *On arriving at Doultons, I found the men — stokers and burners — in the midst of their work, the fires of the kiln, seen from the outside through the fire holes, roaring upwards to the dome-shaped top, then forced downwards so that the smoke, driven to the bottom, escaped beneath the floor through a series of tubes, then by a tall shaft to the open air. A fixed ladder leading to an iron platform circling the dome gave access to the salting-holes.*

Whilst Doulton's kiln of the 1920s was of the down-draught type, it does not help in establishing the design of the kiln in use at Kishere's potworks over one hundred years earlier. In fact, in the absence of archaeological evidence it appears unlikely that the down-draught method of firing pots had been developed before the 1840s. A diagram of the features included in such a kiln are shown in Plate 41, but we have to assume that Joseph Kishere built and used an up-draught kiln with similar features to the type illustrated in Plate 42 and employed by Stephen Green at Lambeth in the 1830s for salt glazing. It has venting holes in the domed roof, allowing heat and sodium oxide to escape early in the salting process, thereby reducing its efficiency. Drawn to a scale of

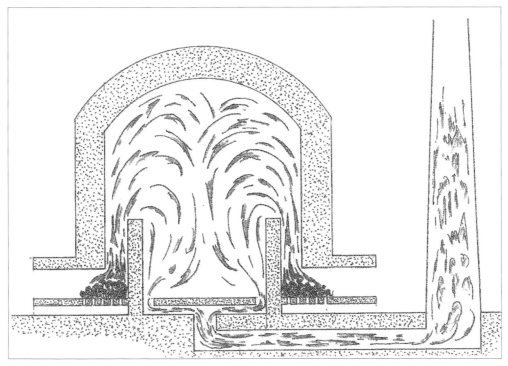

Plate 41. *A diagram illustrating the principles of a theoretical down-draught kiln. Bag walls, rising to approximately half the interior height of the kiln, direct the flames to the dome and the heat and fumes are then drawn down to the flue vents in the base. Heat is evenly distributed between the pots, avoiding any scorching from direct contact with the flames, and a damper in the exit flue or chimney is used to control reduction and oxidation. A high chimney ensures adequate ventilation. It is thought that down-draught kilns were not developed until the mid-1800s.*

DEVISED AND PREPARED BY NIGEL FORBES-MARSDEN

2cm = 1 metre the chimney was over 26ft. (8m) high and the interior of the kiln had a diameter of approximately 7ft.6in. (2.3m) and a maximum height of 6ft.7in. (2m). The essential prerequisites were adequate ventilation to ensure an efficient and even distribution of the sodium oxide vapour, an effective flue and a high chimney to vent the waste products of the chemical reaction. Hydrogen chloride gas forms hydrochloric acid when it comes into contact with water vapour and under similar conditions any surplus sodium oxide forms caustic soda – a potentially hazardous concoction.

From the commissioning of a new kiln its characteristics will change with each successive firing, one of many variables to be taken into consideration by the potter. The vaporised sodium oxide not only combines with the pottery but also attacks the bricks and all surfaces of the kiln, covering them with a glaze if they contain any alumino-silicate material which is usually present to some extent. This residual sodium alumino-silicate gradually builds up and melts with each firing, adding to the effectiveness of the glazing process. A mature kiln requires less salt and will produce a richer glaze than a new kiln. Unfortunately, having reached its peak performance it will then decline slowly but inexorably towards disintegration as the salt continues to attack the fabric of the kiln. Ultimate destruction may be delayed if very high alumina bricks are used in its construction, reducing the assimilation of salt, although it may never have the attributes of a mature kiln. The choice lies between a short life producing good results and a long life producing mediocre results.

Salt (sodium chloride) begins to decompose at a temperature above 1100°C (orange glow) and from this level to 1250°C (yellow glow), and possibly as high as 1300°C (white glow), three to five saltings are injected into the kiln. Joseph Kishere did not have the benefit of a thermocouple and potentiometer capable of giving reasonably precise temperature readings and must therefore have judged the heat by the colour glow of the kiln's interior, viewed through a spyhole. Having decided to commence salting, water – as required in the chemical reaction – is introduced by damping the salt which can be thrown directly into the fireboxes or, as in the case of John Wisker and Doultons, ladled through holes at the head of the kilns. Care is necessary; a wet solution of salt will result in an explosion due to the rapid expansion of excessive steam. The firing programme is monitored with the help of test pieces which are placed adjacent to a removable bung and withdrawn from the kiln at intervals for examination. Using his experience and instinct the potter must judge whether the deposit of sodium oxide on the pots is proceeding satisfactorily or whether further salting will improve the end result.

When considering the type of fuel required for firing Joseph Kishere's kilns we can reduce the choice to either coal or wood. Electricity as a heat source is not compatible with salt glazing, the metal elements being immediately attacked by the the salt; moreover, electric power was not commercially available in London until 1882. Gas produced from coal was marketed in London from 1812 but it was an expensive, impure product and for these reasons coal gas was used mainly for lighting rather than heating.

Blacker mentions that coal was firing Doulton's kilns as late as 1920. Nevertheless, we cannot immediately dismiss wood, an alternative fuel which is much favoured by today's salt glaze studio potters in their search for special effects from flying wood ash settling on the pots and variable flames producing scorchmarks on the surfaces. There are disadvantages, however: the wood has to be completely dry, it must be in small pieces or in off-cuts to increase area in order to generate more heat and the procedure is far more demanding, involving frequent stoking and a lengthier firing programme.

We know that coal was readily available in London and the surrounding villages in the second half of the seventeenth century. Indeed, a coal dealer, based in Mortlake High Street, appears in the 1811 Survey (Appendix 2). Bearing in mind the disadvantages of wood fuel and the unsophisticated pottery manufactured by Joseph Kishere, it is reasonable to assume that coal, readily available in the immediate vicinity, was used to fire his kiln. Whilst saggars (fire proof containers) were used by the Staffordshire potters to protect fine porcelain from grit, smoke and scorch marks, such a precaution would be unnecessary in firing the more robust earthenwares and, in any event, the very nature of salt glazing called for an unhindered flow of gases around the wares. Bag walls or equivalent features protected the pots from scorchmarks and small clay pads or wads were placed under the base of pots to prevent adhesion when stacked on open shelves arranged in tiers around the wall of the kiln.

The composition of the clay has a major influence on the quality of the glaze, its colour and that of the body. Fireclays with aluminium oxide and silica molecular ratios of 1:5 or higher are the most suitable materials for salt glazing. Other things being equal, the lower ratios are likely to produce a pronounced 'orange peel' effect whereas a glassy surface should result from higher ratios. The colour of the fired glaze depends partly on the iron oxide content of the clay. Those clays containing up to 2% iron oxide usually

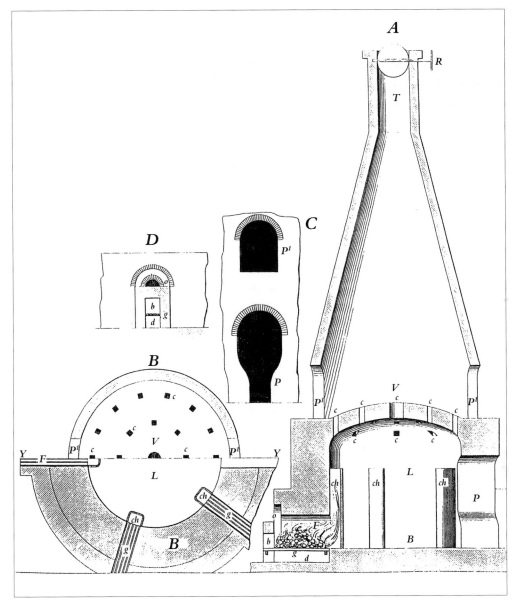

Plate 42. *A free translation of the French key to the above diagram which appears in Alexandre Brongniart's book* Traite des Arts Ceramiques ou des Poteries, *Jeune Bechet, Paris, 1854.*

Kiln for manufacturing grey earthenware at Lambeth, near London, drawn by V. de Pontigny and based on one of the kilns used by Stephen Green. This coal-fired kiln was very similar to the cylindrical kilns built in France and Germany.
A *Vertical perspective through the line* ***YY***.
L *The kiln.*
F *Fire box.* ***b)*** *mouth of the fire box,* ***o)*** *stokehole,* ***d)*** *ash pit,* ***g)*** *fire grate,* ***ch)*** *special chimneys from each fire box directing heat and smoke towards the dome of the kiln and preventing scorching of pots on the lower shelves from direct exposure to the flames.*
V *Dome of the kiln with smoke vents,* ***cc)*** *the central vent is larger than the others.*
P *Kiln access door,* ***P'*** *chimney inspection door,* ***T*** *neck of the chimney,* ***R*** *damper.*
B *Sectional plan of the kiln at the level of the fire grate.*
B' *Sectional plan of the dome of the kiln.*
C *View of the access and inspection doors, P kiln access door, P' inspection door to the kiln dome and chimney.*
D *Front view of the fire box.*
Authors' note: Stephen Green's pottery in Lambeth manufactured earthenware from 1828 to 1831 and stoneware from 1831 to 1858. The products, which were often marked, included general stoneware, blackings, porter bottles, jam jars, jugs and a range of moulded flasks. In 1834 the stone bottle duty amounted to £70.5s.0d.[3]

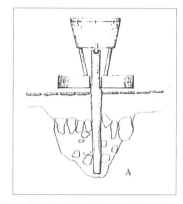

Plate 43b. *A working diagram of an early kick-wheel based on archaeological evidence. The central pivot is embedded in stones below floor level.*

DAVID GAINSTER: *GERMAN STONEWARE 1200-1900*, BRITISH MUSEUM PRESS, LONDON, 1997

Plate 43a. *A potter throwing a pot with the help of a kick-wheel. This woodcut is dated to the 16th century.*
JOST AMMAN *STANDEBUCH [BOOK OF TRADES]*, FRANKFURT-AM-MAIN 1568

take white to tan salt glazes. Brown glazes are produced when the iron oxide content is 3.5% to 4.75% while mahogany coloured glazes can be expected when the iron oxide ratio falls between 4.75% and 8.2%.

Apart from the proportion of iron oxide in the clay, two other factors are equally important, namely the firing temperature and the kiln atmosphere. They can be conveniently dealt with after firstly describing a decorative feature common to Kishere's wares and other contemporary salt glaze potters operating at that time.

Traditionally the salt-glazed mugs, jugs, tobacco jars and other pieces were made in two colours, the lower section being in tan or light brown and the upper section of the vessel finished in a contrasting dark brown produced by dipping the unfired pot in either an iron wash or a clay slip mixed with red ochre (iron oxide). Dipping was done by hand, the inverted mug being held at the base between the fingers and dipped into the iron wash or slip, covering perhaps a third or a half of the outer body. Trapped air within the vessel was partly compressed as the slip entered the interior of the mug, allowing only a narrow band of colour to form beneath the rim on the inner surface when fired.

Assuming the clay used in making the pot contained approximately 2% iron oxide, the lower section of the vessel would have a tan-coloured glazed surface after firing. Adding red ochre to slip, made from the same clay, would increase the iron oxide to say 6% and the upper section would then exhibit the contrasting deep brown/mahogany colour. Achievement of richly textured colours is contingent on the kiln atmosphere and its temperature. During any firing sequence there is a natural cycle of reduction and oxidation. Each time the fires are stoked or salted, smoke and fumes reduce the oxygen within the kiln but when the fires burn clear and hot, more air is drawn in and the atmosphere is enriched with oxygen. A damper, or the removal of loose bricks from air ports, can also be used to control the concentration of oxygen. A reduced oxygen atmosphere turns the iron oxide from red to grey and no doubt Joseph Kishere would have made good use of oxidation and slow cooling to produce the creams, tans and browns featured in his wares.

A contemporary quotation from John Dwight establishes the source of his raw materials in the seventeenth century. Dwight may not have been the first potter to produce salt-glazed stoneware in Britain but he was one of the earliest and the Fulham pottery he established in the 1670s was an undoubted commercial success. He studied chemistry at Oxford and, at a later date, tested and experimented with different clays before starting his own ceramic business. A notebook kept by William Gilpen, who is thought to have been employed by Dwight, gives an insight into the raw materials used at the Fulham pottery and also an outline of their production methods. It reads:

Is made at Fullham 'tis made of White Clay, or Rather of Tobacco pipe Clay, this is brought out of Dorsetshire, it is dug out of the pitts a bout a foot square and so dryed, after that it is Ground with a Stone much like a Syder Mill, afterwards sifted through a fine Sive; and Mixed with a fine smale sort of sand which is brought from the Isle of Wight, after that it's Mixed with water and wrought to a plyable temper, and afterwards put into a pitt, and is there Mixed and wrought well together by treading then it's carried to the Workeing Roome and Moulded like fine paste; after that divided into smale parcells according to the Worke designed for, there being severall sorts, as Juggs, Stone Bottles, Drinking Muggs

Plate 44. *By the 1750s a new but simple development significantly increased the productivity of the thrower. His potting wheel was driven by a rope belt connected to a remote, large wheel turned by a young girl or boy. Efficiency could be further improved by employing a third member of the team to prepare balls of clay ready for use by the thrower.* THE PENNY MAGAZINE, 'A DAY AT THE ROYAL PORCELAIN WORKS', WORCESTER, 1843

&c, they are wrought or turned upon a Blocke with a foot Wheele as Gally Ware, when tis thus Made its sett by to dry, the Roome in which it's dried being built to open on three sides for the more Conveniency of wind and wether, and at the Cloase End there is a long Stoave, in which they put the Ashes and Embers, that comes from their furnaces, which keeps it allwayes warme Especialy when it's shut up cloase. After it's through Dryed it is Leaded and then sett in the Furness, which Furness is built a bout Eight feet square, Arched at the top like a valt with holes to let out the Smooke; in this Furness it is sett or plased a Cloase as maybe one peece by another up to the very top, the smale ware being put in Cases, but the bigger without, under the Furness is the Fier place built the full bigness of the Furness Arched at the top with Brick, with holes, through which the flame Ascends into the Furness.

The Fier is Made wth Wood and burns extreame ferce, to that degree that the inside of the Furness seems to be Leaded over, and they are forced to dig it out of the fier holes with pickaxes.[5]

The importance of Dorset as a source of raw materials for British potteries is illustrated by the quantity of clay exported from Wareham to London, Hull, Liverpool and Glasgow. In the early 1800s it had reached an annual figure of around 10,000 tons. There was considerable rivalry between Wareham and Poole Harbour, the latter port being equally well situated to handle the shipment of white pipe clay found in the Bagshot sands and worked around and to the west of Poole Harbour. Blue clay was dug in the region of Wareham and with its relative purity and natural plasticity was an ideal medium for the fast growing ceramic industry.

Dorset ball-clay and sand may have been the raw materials also used by Joseph Kishere to produce a clay suitable for the potter's wheel. Desmond Eyles[6] summarises a lecture given in 1885 by Doulton's art director to the staff of the Lambeth Art Department from which we learn that Dorset and Devon clays only needed to be ground before adding sand and water. This mix was used at the Doulton pottery for the manufacture of small jugs and pots but for larger articles they added 'grog' (ground-up waste of fired pottery) to give greater stability in the firing.

Although small steam engines were in use by the 1780s, there can be little doubt that Joseph Kishere did not invest in the 'latest technology' and the stables at his pottery point strongly to the use of horse power in turning the grindstone to pulverise the ball-clay. The initial task, however, involved manually breaking the ball-clay with mallets and hammers before the material could be fed into the grinding mill. At the next stage the ground clay needed to be dry sifted to remove unwanted rock fragments and then mixed with sand and water until it reached its full plastic potential. Further preparation may have been necessary to remove any trapped air bubbles in order to create a plastic body ready for moulding or throwing; this could only be accomplished by the laborious task of kneading the clay. It is thought that some of Kishere's wares were press moulded but we are safe in assuming that the major part of his output was created by the hand of a thrower as the clay revolved using a kick-wheel propelled by the potter's feet, or a throwing wheel driven by a belt from a large remote wheel turned by a young boy or girl.

Slip, composed of prepared clay mixed with water into a semi-liquid state with the consistency of cream, was needed for colour dipping after adding iron oxide. It may also have been used as an adhesive for bonding handles and relief figuring, known as sprigging, to the surface of pots although simply dampening the surface and the sprig

Plate 45. *The young lady in the foreground is photographed 'teasing' a sprig out of a plaster of Paris mould, an operation carried out with the help of a spatula. The sprigs were placed on a damp slab in readiness for the ornamentor. c.1905.*

could be equally effective.

A number of methods were available to Joseph Kishere when making ornamentation or ancillary pieces such as handles and some of these entailed the use of clay moulds. The process of sprigging started with an original clay model from which a fired block mould was produced. A 'copy' of the original model could now be created from the block mould although continuous use would dull the sprig's crispness. To avoid deterioration a case mould (positive) was made from which working moulds were produced, for use as and when required. In judging the size of the original model allowance had to be made for the shrinkage of wet to dry clay, plus further contraction as the result of firing the mould itself. Working moulds were fired at a temperature high enough to harden the clay without destroying its absorbent quality.

The stylised sprigging of topers with foaming tankards, trees, cottages, windmills, mounted huntsmen and hounds, foxes and so on decorated the hunting jugs and mugs. To ensure a secure bond between the sprig and the pot Joseph Kishere would have used the same or similar clay for both components. The sprigging procedure begins with a ball of prepared clay from which a thin sheet (batt) is cut with a copper or bronze wire stretched between two widely spaced prongs attached to a single handle. Alternatively the clay sheet could have been made by using a rolling pin, or beaten with a 'batter', a tool resembling a clothes' iron. A piece of clay cut from the batt is then laid across the mould and pressed by finger into every contour of the mould, also ensuring that surplus clay rises above the cavity. If the face of the mould is clean and level, as it should be, any surplus clay can be simply removed with a knife to produce a sprig with a smooth reverse side. The porous mould quickly absorbs water from the damp clay and its slight shrinkage enables the sprig to be removed easily. It is then hand applied to the pot, making sure that the fine detail is preserved and is undamaged by the operator's fingers.

Not all moulds started life as original models. An alternative source of sprigging may seem somewhat unethical, but amongst potters there was a widespread practice of copying applied plaques from dry-bodied Staffordshire stonewares. Everybody copied everybody else, either buying from the same modeller, who made the originals, or copying directly from the pot, when there would be some shrinkage in size on firing the new block mould (negative).

It is known that press-moulded wares, made in two halves, were produced by the Kishere pottery in the later years of its existence and this technique would have played a part in making their 'flat bottles' of which some are marked. There is at least one example of the factory also using the process of slip-casting. Appendix 9 includes illustrations of a spirit flask in the form of a sailor (Plate 66) and two sections of a three-piece mould (D17 in the Church collection) for making such wares. All the moulds have raised and corresponding recessed natches to ensure accurate registration and, being made of plaster of Paris, they absorb some of the water from the clay slip which is poured into a hole at the top. A layer of clay congeals against the inner walls, excess water is poured off, the cast hardens and natural shrinkage facilitates its removal. Slip-casting was not commercially viable until the late nineteenth century when it was found that the quantity of water required in the slip could be significantly reduced by the introduction of soluble alkalis into the mix, known as deflocculation, thus speeding up the process and avoiding the frequent topping-up as the water soaked into the moulds.

The strap handles found on Kishere pots were probably made with the help of a 'dod box'. Soft clay is fed into a cylindrical box and a screw-threaded plunger wound down forcing the clay through a die in the base of the cylinder. The extruded product is a uniform strip of clay with a moulded profile ready for shaping into the form of a handle. Simple decorative features, occasionally seen at the base of mug and jug handles, may have been produced from moulds but they are more likely to have been cut and shaped by hand.

Another form of traditional decoration which featured on the earlier Kishere jugs consisted of a series of parallel grooves or 'ribbing' around the neck, produced by turning the ware in its 'greenhard' state on a lathe with the body of the jug held in a hollow drum. The most expensive jugs were finished with lidded mounts in silver or pewter. In adding the pewter mounts it is possible that our potter patronised a local craftsman, William Watson, whose name is annotated as a whitesmith in the 1811 Survey (Appendix 2). As well as working with tin he may have applied his skills to pewter, an alloy of tin and lead. However, the making and fitting of silver mounts is more likely to have been contracted to a London silversmith.

If the potter has mastered all the variables of salt glazing correctly, the end product should be a strong and durable stoneware pot of a dense and highly vitrified clay covered in a hard, non-porous, chemical resistant glaze fused with the body and sufficiently thin and transparent to leave the relief moulding unobscured. Compared with the production

Plate 46. *A photograph of Thomas Lovatt, a prestige ornamentor, working on a jasper copy of the Portland vase. The quality and sharpness of the bas-relief depended on the skill of his craftsmanship. c.1905.*

of china and porcelain, which require a sequence of firings including biscuit, glost, enamel, gilding and so on, the process of salt glazing is completed in a single firing. As a result the pottery is produced economically and quickly, ideal qualities for a small provincial potter with modest resources at his disposal and supplying a limited market.

It does seem appropriate to close this chapter with a contemporary account of salt glazing, particularly when the authority quoted is John Wisker who, as mentioned earlier, ran his business from Sanders' Mortlake pottery from 1809 to 1823, production being transferred to Lambeth at this latter date. *Illustrations of Arts and Manufactures*[7] includes the transcript of a lecture given by Mr. A. Aikin to the Society for the Encouragement of Arts, Manufactures and Commerce in 1829 and is quoted below:

A more perfect, and indeed very excellent species of earthenware, is that called stoneware, originally introduced from Holland and now made in several parts of the kingdom and especially at Lambeth. To one of the principal manufacturers of this ware, Mr. Wisker, I am indebted for the specimens on the table, and for the following particulars.

The materials are, pipe-clay from Dorsetshire and Devonshire, calcinated and ground flint from Staffordshire, and sand from Woolwich and Charlton.

The clay is pulverised and sifted dry, and is either used alone, when an article of great compactness is required, as soda-bottles, or is mixed with sand to diminish its contraction in the fire. For retorts and other large vessels, instead of sand, the refuse stone ware, ground to a fine powder, is used. For other finer articles, such as figured jugs, ground flint is employed instead of sand. The composition is brought about by the addition of water, to the state of mortar, and is then tempered in the pug-mill. All round articles are made on the horizontal wheel; and those of great size, i.e., of a greater capacity than two gallons, are at first of extraordinary thickness below to support the upper part; when they come off the wheel they are dried, and then are put on a lathe and shaved down to the proper thickness. For oval and other figures not circular, as pans for salting hams in, the clay is formed in a mould to the required shape. The drying, especially of large articles, must be very carefully performed; and as, from custom, the tops or bottoms of jars and various other vessels made of this ware are required to be of a deeper brown than the natural colour of the materials, they are dipped so far in a mixture of red ochre and clayslip. When perfectly dry they are piled in the furnace, bits of well-sanded clay being put between each piece to prevent them from adhering. A slow fire is kept up for twelve to twenty-four hours, according to the thickness of the ware, capable of bringing it just to a low red heat. The fire is then to be raised till the flame and the ware are of the same colour, and it is to be continued for several hours. At this time the glaze is added, which is done by pouring down the holes at the top of the kiln, twenty or thirty in number, ladlefuls of common salt. This being volatilised by the intense heat of the interior, attaches itself to the surface of the ware; here it is decomposed, the muriatic acid flying off, and the soda remaining behind in union with the earth with which it forms a very thin, but on the whole, a perfect glaze; at least quite sufficient, with the compactness of the ware, to render it completely proof against the percolation, not only of water, but of the strongest acids. So perfect, indeed is the texture of the best ware now made, that it has of late been very largely used in the construction of distillatory vessels for manufacturing chemists, instead of green glass, as being less frangible, and also cheaper. Pickling jars, and many other vessels in which acid substances for food or condiment are kept, as also those earthenware vessels in which great strength is required, are best made of stone ware. Vauxhall is the chief seat of this manufacture near London, where are now about eight houses engaged in this fabric, most of which are actively employed, as the use of it is considerably on the increase.

Chapter Four

KISHERE STONEWARES

By the end of the eighteenth century the English salt-glazed stoneware industry was in a state of flux, the main cause undoubtedly being the huge expansion of the Staffordshire potteries and their markets after the perfection of cream-coloured earthenware by Josiah Wedgwood in the 1760s. This had partially eroded the market for stoneware beer mugs which, along with the more expensive and more stealable pewter, had been the staple furnishing of taverns throughout the country. Creamware beer mugs became common, and much more so after about 1780 when the development of overglaze printing had enabled them to become vehicles for satire and political comment. The bluish 'pearlware' that followed also provided blue transfer-printed beer mugs, to be joined by the hugely popular lathe-turned 'banded' and 'Mocha Ware' in the 1790s. Cheap, clean and hygienic, with a smooth lead-glazed lip and sturdy body and handle, these mugs – banded with coloured slips – continued to be mass produced in the neighbourhood of that great brewing centre, Burton-on-Trent, for the following 150 years.

These developments had in turn put the Nottingham mug makers out of business – the last pottery being closed by 1800 – and had left a large gap in the repertoire of the stoneware potteries of Lambeth and Bristol. Of the staple heavy duty products, drain-pipes and sanitary fittings were certainly made in Lambeth, for they are listed in the London Potters' Price Agreement of 1795, but it was to be some forty years before the typhoid epidemics led to the hasty, widespread adoption of proper sanitation in cities. Bottles were still made in large quantities, particularly the large spirit bottles which could be made in sizes up to four or five gallons – perhaps representing the heaviest weight of ceramic bottle that a man could lift by its handle. But the huge demand for stoneware bottles for ginger beer, blacking and 'blue' (for whitening yellow laundry) and for jam jars for export to the Empire arose only in the first decades of the nineteenth century. When the opportunity for prosperity did come, different potteries tended not to compete directly but to concentrate on different products which offered a better chance of profit. Thus mass-production of heavy drain-pipes suited the London riverside potteries with their export markets, but not the land-locked factories of Derbyshire. Similarly, small bottles could be made at a phenomenal rate by cheap female labour in Derbyshire, in large potteries situated near the excellent stoneware clay and coal which were found together, whereas in London labour was more expensive and all the materials had to be imported.

It might appear, therefore, that the years around 1800 were the worst time to found a new stoneware pottery along the Thames. There were few export markets and in any case the current war with Napoleon would have restricted trade to India, Australia or Canada. With the gradual refinement of pottery and table manners, fewer people wanted to drink from rough salt-glazed tavern mugs. And lastly, the import of expensive clay and coal by a pottery on the Thames could only be justified by the expectation of a large and regular output which would turn a profit as well as cover the overheads: in other words, a well-organised urban pottery operating in company with several others, perhaps sharing common sources of supply for coal from the North East and clay from the South West.

Yet there was a niche in the market, where a small pottery operating as a family business might make attractive decorated stonewares, modestly priced objects which would appeal to both the London and the country market, combining the virtues of tough stoneware with good potting, smooth clay, brilliant glaze and a range of fashionable neo-classical motifs borrowed from contemporary industrial creamwares and white porcellanous stonewares. Indeed, this niche not only bridged the gap between the coarse, gritty eighteenth century Lambeth or Fulham stonewares and the refined banded earthenwares of the Midlands, but its growth was assured by the nostalgic reaction amongst British beer drinkers against those mechanically perfect but uninteresting white beer mugs which threatened to deprive them of the three hundred year bond between ale and brown stoneware. If the British love of rural sports could also be catered for, in the manner of those giant hunting mugs made intermittently in London and Bristol for pubs and drinking clubs throughout the eighteenth century, then success would be certain. Though such a small enterprise might be overshadowed by the large potteries in Fulham and Lambeth belching coal smoke and chlorine gases into the surrounding squalid streets from their many bottle-ovens, its highly specialised products should hardly intrude upon their trade, but instead should establish a new market for the re-launch and up-dating of an old product.

Whether or not Joseph Kishere (8) considered all these points is impossible to know. What we do know is that his father Benjamin (1) had risen to become foreman at the delftware and stoneware pottery of John Sanders in Mortlake High Street and that some time shortly after his father's death in 1780 the young Joseph was apprenticed to Sanders & Vernon. After serving his seven years, he probably worked a further ten years at the pottery before deciding to set up a pottery of his own, allegedly after acquiring capital through an advantageous marriage and a win in the State Lottery. There are several clues to the date when the pottery was founded: Joseph probably acquired enough capital after his marriage in 1795 and many pots attributed to Kishere have silver mounts hallmarked to the late 1790s, but a definite date of 1797 is established by the rate books (Appendix 1) which, in that year, record a move from East Sheen Lane (to the High Street) and the temporary housing of 'potters' in his former property. Though Joseph was trained in both delftware and stoneware production, by this period there was barely enough demand from the pharmaceutical trade for delftware ointment pots (Plate 49) to justify its con-tinued manufacture by Sanders' pottery. Instead he chose to specialise in making sprig-decorated brown stonewares of the type already being made at the Sanders pottery, most

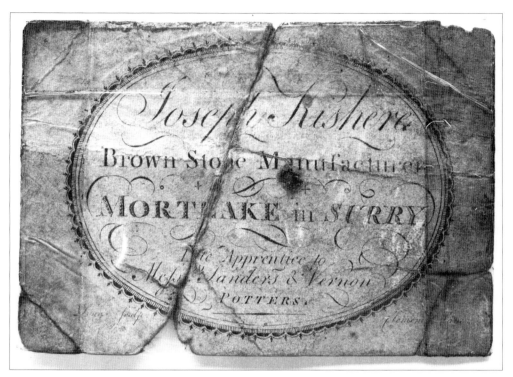

Plate 47. *Trade card for 'Joseph Kishere Brown Stone Manufacturer MORTLAKE in SURRY Late Apprentice to Messrs Sanders and Vernon POTTERS'. Signed 'L…sculp.' and 'Clemen…'.* MORTLAKE CHURCH COLLECTION

probably taking moulds from his former employer to get production started. It was, in any case, inevitable that there should be overlapping of styles and decoration between the two competing potteries. To judge from the number of surviving products, the Kishere pottery thrived but probably lacked the potential to expand. By 1811 it was described in Lyson's *Supplement* as a 'small manufactory of white stone-ware'. Though never white, apart from some unique pieces now at Mortlake Church, Kishere's pots may well have seemed cream coloured when compared with the dense chocolate brown of the common stonewares of Nottingham and Derbyshire, or the rough, gritty products of Lambeth and Fulham.

Practically no details are known of the workings of the Kishere pottery. However, a tantalising glimpse of Kishere's dealings is to be found on the back of his trade card (Plate 47) which (as was common practice) has been used as a receipt: 'Received the 13th April 1818 two Crates for Mr Pathen Lewis, The George Inn, Borough'. This famous sixteenth century Southwark coaching inn, which had already been completely re-built to its original form after a serious fire, may have been buying considerable quantities of traditional (not to say archaic) beer mugs and jugs from the pottery. But no account books or records survive and it is only from the evidence of the pots themselves, from the scant contemporary references and from published scraps of folk memory that we are able to build up a picture of the business. In 1817 Sir Richard Phillips, in his walk to Kew, describes viewing a 'manufactory of Delft and stone-ware' for which 'among potters' Mortlake was famous, and recounts his difficulties in gaining admission to the workshop where its secret processes might be discovered. The pottery is further described as employing a dozen workmen at 20s. (£1) a week, with the implication that such a low wage would not guarantee the safety of any valuable pottery secrets. The pottery that Sir Richard visited was clearly the Sanders establishment, particularly as he mentions a kiln for brown and another for white (a traditional description for delftware). Thus we may infer that the Kishere pottery was on an even smaller scale, perhaps employing some of Joseph Kishere's children, the eldest of whom would have been twenty-one at the time. Confirmation of the family's involvement in the pottery comes from John Eustace Anderson's statement that Joseph's sons William (26) and John Griffin (33) were brought up to the pottery business, and further that Susan (29), born 1805, used to help stamp out the hunting sprigs. One may picture a pottery with a single kiln, the men throwing the hunting jugs which Sir Richard Phillips considered to be the main product of the Mortlake potters, while the women pressed clay into the plaster moulds, teased the little sprigs out of their shallow depressions and, after brushing the backs with clay slip, picked them up with the point of a knife and placed them accurately upon the jugs. As for the labour-intensive parts of pottery production, such as clay preparation and managing not only the firing of the kiln but the critical process of salting, we may conclude from the highly refined body of the Kishere's stoneware that they imported excellent material from the West Country, uncorrupted by blending with coarse clays, and that the kiln was small enough to be controlled by one or two firemen who were prepared to lose a night's sleep. The scale of the pottery would have been carefully designed to produce commercial success with the minimum of manpower, but it is impossible to guess at the number of employees. We should, however, remember that later in the nineteenth century the four Martin Brothers managed all their processes themselves, from throwing and modelling to kiln-firing.

If we use the marked Kishere products as a barometer for the firm's prosperity, then Joseph Kishere's death in 1834 brought little if any change to the pottery's production. The fact that the works were bequeathed to William alone, and that his brother John Griffin was compelled to abandon a lifetime of potting to seek employment as a carter and drayman at the local brewery, speaks of a firm barely able to support its owner and his dependents. By this time, of course, hunting jug production was in full swing at the Fulham Pottery and at many potteries in Lambeth, and the range of decorated stoneware made in Derbyshire was expanding all the time. Simultaneously, mass-production of cheap Staffordshire pottery from the 1830s onwards – for example, moulded and self-coloured stoneware jugs of an almost infinite range of designs – probably helped to push rustic salt glaze further down the social scale. If the Mortlake pottery was now forced to compete directly with those of Lambeth and elsewhere, it could not hope to survive. And, in fact, the marked and dated stonewares of the 1830s and 1840s have little to distinguish them from other contemporary stonewares, either in shape, colour or in their very conventional sprigged decoration. Before the full effect of competition could be felt, however, the fate of the pottery was decided by the early death of William Kishere in 1843, when the business was closed forthwith and offered for sale by his widow.

With hindsight it might appear that the Kishere pottery had outlived its usefulness and profitability and that its imminent closure could have been predicted. Many small country potteries making lead-glazed earthenwares did manage to survive throughout the nineteenth century but these were not competing directly against major industrialised firms and, with the advent of the Arts & Crafts Movement, these 'craft' potteries benefited from a renewed interest in hand-made rustic pottery. In the field of stoneware production, the 1840s was a period of rapid expansion when new products and new markets were developed, notably for gin-flasks, bottles of all kinds, water-filters, chemical stonewares, sanitary wares and also terracotta, the new tough but decorative cladding material which appealed so much to Victorian architects from the mid-nineteenth century onwards. Production on this scale would have been impossible at the small Kishere pottery, even with a major financial investment. But in Lambeth, with growing prosperity and the building of the Embankment in 1866-70, the small riverside potteries amalgamated, grew and became more efficient to keep up with the huge demand for their products. For example, when James Stiff took over the London pottery in Lambeth High Street in 1846, he is stated by Llewellynn Jewitt to have had two kilns on a quarter-acre site, but by 1878 he had fourteen kilns on a two-acre site with a private dock under the Embankment. The firm Doulton & Watts took over the Lambeth Pottery, also in the High Street, in 1827 and expanded rapidly until by 1878 they employed 600 men and consumed 10,000 tons of coal per annum. It is doubtful whether William Kishere would have been able to survive for long in the face of such local competition.

The subsequent history of the pottery after William Kishere's death, though brief, is both interesting and revealing. In 1845 the site was acquired by Thomas Abbott, a resident of Richmond and builder by trade, who moved with his family to Mortlake some years later. His younger brother, John Abbott, described himself as a tallow dealer in the 1841 census return for Richmond where he lived and traded from premises in Hill Street. Following negotiations between the two brothers John obtained a lease of the pottery with the intention of setting-up his eighteen year old son, Thomas Abbott, as a maker of slipware baking dishes. This in itself may appear odd at first sight but the steady demand for these wares is confirmed by dealers' advertisements of the period which include 'Sunderland Ware' and so-called Welsh Trays – both names for trailed slipware dishes, which had by no means gone out of fashion after the perfection of cheap Staffordshire white earthenwares. The few attributable Abbott dishes, clearly stamped on the back 'Abbott Potter' (Plate 25), 'Abbott Mortlake Pottery' or uniquely 'ABBOTT MORTLAKE POTTERY WARRANTED FIRE PROOF', in printer's type, show Thomas Abbott to have been a highly competent slipware potter certainly as good as any potters from the traditional slipware-making areas of the North and the North Midlands. Nevertheless the Mortlake venture lasted for only two years and there are a number of possible reasons for its demise, including Anderson's equivocal statement that 'the pottery did not seem to answer', as young Mr. Thomas's uncle resumed possession of the premises. On the other hand, perhaps the net income from manufacturing a good but very cheap article on such a small scale was inadequate to pay the rent charged by his uncle as well as provide a living or, perhaps, the attraction of a much better return on his original investment may have persuaded Thomas the builder to convert the site into several dwellings. John Abbott, now describing himself as a potter, was evidently undeterred by the Mortlake closure and by 1849 had leased from Joanna Goulding the pottery at Hounslow, formerly the Isleworth pottery where slipware dishes had been made from the end of the eighteenth century, and where surviving accounts of 1792-1805 list large quantities supplied to London dealers at sixpence or sevenpence each, providing a modest but regular profit. Here John Abbott continued the production of slipware dishes until about 1855 when the pottery closed. Throughout this period he also continued trading from his Richmond warehouse having added china, glass and probably slipware to his stock-in-trade and, assuming his son Thomas was pursuing a new career, John Abbott may have recruited a pottery foreman and experienced hands from the redundant Isleworth workforce.

Returning to the heyday of the Mortlake potteries, the evidence of surviving pots does nothing to contradict the traditional assumption that Mortlake was the birthplace of the stoneware hunting jug. However, since the original Sanders pottery and its newer Kishere rival were running in parallel during the period 1797 to 1823, the isolation of the two potteries' products is not a straightforward matter. In view of the number of excavated pharmaceutical wares we may suppose that Sanders concentrated on containers at least as much as blue-painted tin-glazed tablewares, and of the early stonewares likely to have been made at Mortlake, we may therefore single out those globular beer bottles which were a standard product of all the London stoneware potteries. Strong circumstantial support for the production of these is provided by the discovery of fragments of two beer bottles at Carter's Grove, Virginia, bearing an applied medallion with the moulded inscription: 'G:Burwell/Edwd Atthaws/1755' (Plate 48), matched on a surviving intact bottle in an American collection. Extensive documentation about Carter's Grove estate shows that the owner, Carter Burwell, completed a large new mansion there in 1755 (also the year of his death) and that the London agent who converted his tobacco crop into cash was Edward Athawes. One of the plausible explanations for the two names on the bottle medallion is that Edward Athawes may have sent out bottled ale as a gift to his friend and employer, perhaps to celebrate the completion of his new house in that year. Edward Athawes' property was rated at a sizeable 'rent' of £14 in the Mortlake Poor Rate Books of 1754-5, and there is abundant evidence that the Athawes and Sanders families knew each other well. Firstly Athawes' name appears on a list of members of the Society of Arts proposed by Sanders' partner in the porcelain venture, Nicholas Crisp, and secondly William Sanders appointed Samuel Athawes as trustee in his will of 1780, which was witnessed by Edward Athawes, presumably son of Edward Athawes Snr. who was buried at Mortlake Church in 1767. It is entirely reasonable, therefore, to suppose that 'special order' stoneware bottles would have been commissioned from the local pottery owned by Athawes' friend. It may also be significant that two slightly earlier stoneware beer bottles in the Museum of London are inscribed 'Topham' (Plate 5), the name of an established brewing family which became well known in Mortlake during the nineteenth century. Final confirmation that bottles were made there comes from the finding of a bottleneck waster of mid-eighteenth century type during demolition of the Sanders 'Malthouse' in 1997, together with body fragments from larger spirit bottles.

In 1795 Thomas Norris, who had taken over the Sanders pottery the year before, was signatory to a price-fixing declaration which listed the standard utilitarian wares made by London potteries. Although we do not know whether his Mortlake pottery made all the wares listed, the document does provide a good indication of the directions in which

Plate 48. *Stoneware bottle with medallion moulded with 'G. Burwell. Edwd. Atthaws 1755'.* **Sanders** *factory.*   WILLIAMSBURG

a medium-sized pottery, having reduced its delftware production to a minimum, might have expanded its stoneware capabilities. The bulk of the items were bottles, jars and gorges (originally globular mugs but by this time almost certainly jugs of similar form), special bottles for spruce beer and liquid blue, barrels and 'Shop Pots' (large display or storage jars). The few items for drainage listed at the end evidently did not then form a major part of the London stoneware potters' production.

As for decorated wares, other probable Sanders products are the tall beer jugs covered with sprigged hunting figures which, on the evidence of an example with silver mount of 1793 engraved 'Success to Fox hunting', may well have been used at hunt suppers. So many of these survive, in many different sizes, that they must have been produced in large numbers while those having silver mounts with hallmarks earlier than the founding of the Kishere pottery in 1797 must inevitably be attributed to the Sanders pottery. The earliest hallmarked mounts of 1783 (private collection) and 1786 (National Museum & Gallery on Merseyside, the date engraved on the silver rim, Plate 17), both with the square 'Punch Party' plaque and rather globular body with terraced footrim, recall the large beer jugs made in Southwark and Lambeth from the early eighteenth century onwards which were very occasionally inscribed and decorated with hunting figures like those well-known series of giant hunting mugs dated between 1713 and at least 1775. A handful of comparable jugs with this 'fat' profile have survived (for example, two in the Museum of London, one of which is much battered and repaired in tin, and another hallmarked 1793 at Sotheby's Olympia, 5.4.2002), but the majority are of the later baluster type, typified by the small example with domed silver lid in Sheffield Museum dated 1795 (Plate 38) or the more waisted example with rounded footrim dated 1799 (private collection, Plate 30). Notable individual sprigs found on these jugs are the rectangular plaques of the 'Punch Party', the two boors drinking (after Teniers, and often flanked by classical figures), the 'Cupids' Procession' (modelled for Wedgwood by Hackwood and much copied by other potters), an oval plaque of a racehorse being saddled (possibly after Stubbs, and also found on later squat jugs), a small figure of Fame blowing her trumpet, a dancing cupid with tambourine raised above the head (after Wedgwood), the post-type windmill also found on later marked Kishere jugs, tall oak trees, a sportsman with shotgun and dead game (found on mugs with rims of 1794 and 1798), two sportsmen shooting pheasants, a dog emerging from a cottage and a pointer beside a tree (also found on later squat jugs). Rare examples of 'the 'Cupids' Procession' incorporating profile portraits of King George III and Queen Caroline may usefully be dated to 1786 (Plate 18), the Silver Jubilee year, or just possibly 1789 when the restoration of the King's sanity was widely commemorated.

The demise of the wheel-thrown baluster jug suggested by the latest dated mount of 1799 might be seen as heralding the introduction of jugs moulded in two halves (Plate 50), based on contemporary Staffordshire 'Pratt' ware jugs with their borders of acanthus leaves and flowers at top and bottom. These share the same decoration as the thrown jugs and are so closely related that it is difficult to believe that they are not simply a development by the Sanders pottery of the earlier type. They are, however, uncommon enough to suggest a brief period of production, these changes in design and technique perhaps having been stimulated by the founding of Kishere's rival pottery in the last years of the century. The rare thrown jugs of this shape – high-shouldered with ribbed or plain necks and all bearing typical Mortlake sprigs – were perhaps made shortly after 1804 when the pottery was acquired by Wagstaff, for a fragmentary undecorated jug of exactly this type was excavated from his former pottery at Vauxhall Cross in 1969-70.

When considering the overlapping of products it must be said that there is no reason why Kishere should not have simply used the familiar Sanders moulds to make identical stoneware at his new pottery. However, a neat solution may be proposed whereby Kishere continued using the Sanders sprig moulds but applied them to a new range of squat hunting jugs – of which those very rare examples marked 'J★K' (Plate 32) are probably the first. The Sanders pottery may then have abandoned the old baluster jugs and attempted to compete first by using cheaper moulding methods and then by copying Kishere's low globular jugs, which were doubtless inspired by the Staffordshire 'Dutch' jugs then coming into fashion. Whatever the sequence of events, the late

Plate 49. *Biscuit delftware ointment pots in salt-glazed saggar.* **Sanders** *factory, probably late 18th century.*

eighteenth century stonewares are of considerable interest in that they not only provide models for Kishere's new pottery but they may well have been made by Kishere himself before he left the Sanders factory.

Very many London type hunting jugs of the 1800-1820 period survive, but from the fact that Messrs Doulton & Watts, one of the few potteries known to have listed hunting jugs amongst their products (in 1818), was only founded in 1815, and that the only hunting jug fragments excavated at the Fulham pottery dated from no earlier than the 1820s, we may deduce that Mortlake then led the field by making the majority of these early examples. In the absence of marks, however, it is hazardous to divide such groups or to make tentative attributions. Even those which share sprigs and other characteristics with supposed Sanders products, though they sometimes fall into neat categories, do not appear to relate to 'phases' of production represented by the various changes of ownership of the Sanders pottery in 1794, 1802, 1804, and 1809. The form of the windmills on hunting jugs has long been considered idiosyncratic, yet at Mortlake even the well-known post-windmill of marked Kishere jugs makes its appearance on supposedly Sanders products.

Given the comparatively limited range of sprigs used on marked Kishere wares and the much larger size and longer life of the Sanders pottery, the number of differing jugs of general Mortlake type is not so surprising. Working from a large number of photographs it is possible to pick out certain recurring sprigs which are not found on marked Kishere pieces and which – always assuming that they are indeed Mortlake – should be products of the Sanders pottery. These are sometimes datable from silver mounts and consist of, amongst others, a pointer facing left under a tree, hanging bunches of grapes, detached figure of a putto from the 'Cupids' Procession' (all on a mug of 1806), oval plaque of racehorse, oval plaque of cock crowing on dunghill in farmyard (both jugs, 1806), square plaque of chickens being fed in a farmyard (jug 1808), the figure of Fame with her trumpet, the dog emerging from a cottage, a square plaque with figures in a tavern interior (jug 1809), and windmills of Type III and IV (see Appendix 5).

The very limited range of dates from these silver mounts is curious and may be explained by the fact that these were added by the retailer (see the Account Books of Thomas Goode, mentioned below); this in turn would reflect the demands of the customer and the changing whims of fashions. The practice of embellishing salt-glazed stoneware drinking vessels extended back to the mid-sixteenth century when imported Rhineland mugs, costing a penny or two, were given elaborate silver-gilt mounts costing over £1. Examples of the seventeenth century were plainer, consisting of lidless mounts engraved with border patterns and sometimes initials, a tradition which was carried on and applied to the new products of John Dwight of Fulham from the 1680s to the beginning of the eighteenth century. As mentioned below, towards the end of the eighteenth century a growing distaste for the mechanical perfection of Staffordshire creamware brought a revival of silver-mounted brown stoneware amongst prosperous or antiquarian beer drinkers. The popularity of this fashion may be deduced from the fact that Staffordshire white stoneware jugs made by Turner, Adams and others, often with mounts and domed lids of the 1790s, were made deliberately rustic with ribbed necks coated in brown slip and applied hunting and Toby figures, reversing the usual trend. It would seem clear that these industrialised potteries were attempting to imitate traditional salt-glazed stonewares. There were few silver mounted after about 1810, and similarly there was evidently no demand for brown stoneware with lids of the new Britannia Metal and electroplate in the 1830s-40s. It was only towards the end of the nineteenth century that the spreading influence of the Arts and Crafts movement made Doulton brown stonewares acceptable at any social level and led to mugs and three-handled loving cups being mounted as prizes for archery societies and other traditional sports.

Though not always marked, sufficient marked Kishere specimens survive to make possible an approximate typology. Early hunting jugs were usually squat with short ribbed neck and a large central plaque, generally the 'Punch Party', the two boors drinking or the 'Cupids' Procession' in square or lunette form, usually flanked by classical figures either in silhouette or on oval pads, all borrowed from Sanders. Some attempt was also made by the Kisheres to copy other sprigs from the large repertoire of decoration designed for Wedgwood's jasper ware, resulting in a truly comical medallion of a massive cupid being pulled by diminutive rat-like lions, flanked by burly cupids in ovals; no hunting jugs with these amusing plaques are actually marked but they appear on one of the early nineteenth century marked white stoneware goblets in Mortlake Church (Plate 51), and a squat jug (Sotheby's Olympia 5.4.2002) with domed silver lid hallmarked 1806. One of the flanking cupids appears on an unmarked jug with a mount of 1806, which seems to have been a popular year for silver mounting. Later these plaques were replaced by a large central figure of the portly Sir Toby Philpot with his foaming tankard, which was probably adopted by potters as bas-relief decoration when the popularity of the three-dimensional Toby jug began to wane in the early nineteenth century. A popular

Plate 50. *Hunting jug, moulded in two halves in imitation of contemporary 'Pratt' ware. Probably* **Sanders** *factory, about 1800-1810. H.5½in. (14cm).*   COURTESY OF THE MINET LIBRARY

form of decoration on Kishere jugs of the 1800-1810 period was a continuous frieze of 'The Meet', common on Staffordshire white stonewares of the early years of the nineteenth century, and for which a mould survives in Mortlake Church (Appendix 9, D18).

Unhappily for historians, the mounts on later Kishere jugs seem to have been mainly Sheffield plate – or alternatively, as so often happened, the original silver mounts may have been sent for scrap. None the less, after the squat jug shapes of the early years of the nineteenth century it is possible to detect later phases of development, the first of which is an elegant jug body with pronounced angular shoulder and small bead foot, a marked example of which (Sotheby's New York 30.11.84) has the 'Cupids' Procession' in a lunette flanked by cut-out classical figures and a silver mount of 1817. An unmarked Kishere jug in the Museum of London, impressed 'T & E BOYS 1820' with Type II windmill and flaring neck and tapering base (Plate 27), indicates that by 1820 the pottery had resigned itself to making entirely conventional shapes. Thereafter, the smooth refined stoneware body, thin potting, solid dark-brown dip, small sprigs and full marking

Plate 51. *Two white stoneware goblets decorated with curious, oversized cherubs and conventional hunting sprigs. Left (C11) probably* **Kishere**. *H. 7½in. (19cm) c.1805-10. Right (C10) impressed mark* **'Kishere Mortlake'**. *H. 7in. (17.8cm) c.1805-10.* MORTLAKE CHURCH COLLECTION

'KISHERE POTTERY MORTLAKE SURRYs' make these jugs barely distinguishable from those of other London stonewares, and indicate dates in the 1830s-40s. We may point to the windmills of Types II, V and VI as reliable indicators of Kishere manufacture, with Types V and VI probably falling into the period when William took over the pottery on his father's death in 1834.

A valuable pointer to the technical expertise and artistic development achieved by the Kishere pottery in the years around 1829 has just come to light. The jug (Plate 51A and Appendix 10), sturdily potted in typical 'Dutch' shape, has no hunting figures but instead is covered with applied vine leaves of the type favoured by contemporary Staffordshire potters as friezes for the necks, shoulders and rims of their white stoneware jugs and porter mugs. It is also found on Bristol stonewares of the 1820s and appears later as a handle terminal on Denby hunting jugs. On the Kishere jug, however, multiple sprigs from one or two moulds have been cut and arranged to fit over the entire surface, including the back of the handle, apparently with the intention of demonstrating the potting skills of the Kishere family members for the base is inscribed 'Made by William Kishere Figured by Fanny Nov. 25 1829'. At this date William was twenty-nine years old (and five years away from inheriting the pottery) whilst his sister Frances (31), a teacher also known as Fanny, had celebrated her twenty-first birthday just a month or two earlier. This tends to confirm Anderson's statement that 'William was brought up to the pottery business' as well as his comments about differing windmill sprigs being applied by individual members of the Kishere family. It is interesting to compare the vine leaf

Plate 51a. A typical squat 'Dutch' shaped jug covered with vine leaves and grapes. Inscribed on the base 'Made by William Kishere Figured by Fanny Nov. 25 1829' (illustrated). H. 7¼in. (18.4cm) c.1805-10. See pages 143-144 for colour illustrations.
PRIVATE COLLECTION

decoration with that on a squat Kishere hunting jug illustrated by J.F. Blacker[1] and the R.P. Alvin mug of 1830 (Plate 19), the three known examples thus including a family memento and a specially commissioned piece. The Kisheres do seem to have been the only stoneware potters in the London area at this period making such 'one-offs' and, given the small size of the pottery, we may conclude that this specialist market was one upon which their survival depended.

Apart from the hunting jugs, which were undoubtedly used for beer, the Mortlake potteries specialised in sprigged beer mugs. Evidently intended for the home, and never marked with the official 'WR' excise mark for tavern use, these highly decorative mugs were made in pint, quart and three pint sizes, of which the quart is perhaps the most common. Following closely the decoration of the baluster jugs, the earliest mug bears a mount of 1784, and the latest 1798 (Plate 28). Thus the same observations apply to these as to the jugs, which is to say, they could have been made by both potteries, or by Kishere when employed by Sanders.

Also closely linked to these mugs and the baluster jugs are the loving cups, notably handsome objects which represent a unique contribution by Mortlake to the range of late eighteenth century English brown stonewares. Of the half dozen or so in museums and private collections, most appear to have been thrown by the same hand, so similar are their forms and, in particular, their feet. Some are equipped with strap handles very like the mugs, others are more like goblets. Many also have Sheffield plate mounts, an example in the collection of Merseyside Museums even having metal handles attached

Plate 52. *Loving cup or goblet, with 'Drunken Boors' and 'Punch Party' plaques, both flanked by classical figures. Inscribed 'JMA' on Sheffield plate mount with metal handles attached to the rim and a strap round the stem. Probably* **Kishere** *factory, about 1800. H. 9in. (23cm). The decoration is almost identical to the slightly smaller loving cup in Plate 36.*
COURTESY OF THE NATIONAL MUSEUMS AND GALLERIES ON MERSEYSIDE M2186

to the rim and to a strap around the stem (Plate 52), but a plain example with a silver mount, at Hanley Museum, unfortunately bears only the maker's mark 'WK' without a date letter. These goblets and loving cups, which copied the form of glass rummers of the 1790-1810 period, apparently cover the same span as the mugs and baluster jugs and thus could have been made at the Sanders and Kishere potteries. A goblet with decoration of supposedly Sanders type and a silver rim hallmarked 1803 has been noted.

The other Mortlake speciality was the tobacco jar, a form which was probably also invented by the Mortlake potteries. The long history of tobacco consumption and storage in Europe is complex and suffice it to say that in England the expensive cylindrical porcelain tobacco pots with lids, used by the wealthy of both sexes, made at Meissen, Mennecy, St. Cloud and Sèvres, were unknown, or at least not replicated by English porcelain manufacturers. To judge from engravings depicting smokers, tobacco was always packaged by tobacconists in small paper parcels, labelled and sealed with wax.

There are few tobacco pots of any material known in England before the late eighteenth century, and certainly not in salt-glazed stoneware. Despite a superficial similarity it is pretty certain that any resemblance between the lidded Continental porcelains of the 1725-75 period and the cylindrical Mortlake pots with their domed lids is coincidental; both were absolutely functional and the Mortlake potteries, having limited facilities for moulding or copying the cast lead tobacco boxes of the early nineteenth century, merely chose the simplest form. These pots, which are often quaintly marked 'Kishere Moatlake' (Plate 37) came in at least two different sizes and have almost always lost their lids. Whether or not they originally had sliding inner lids to keep the contents compacted and fresh, as their cylindrical form would suggest, is uncertain. An occasional pot survives with a windmill of Type III which may well be the Sanders factory. Following these pioneering pots, towards the middle of the nineteenth century, the Brampton potteries in Derbyshire, notably S. & H. Briddon, made a great speciality of fancy moulded, honey-coloured tobacco boxes equipped with inner sliding tampers.

These common stonewares were undoubtedly cheap and, in the absence of a staple mass-produced product such as sanitary wares or storage vessels, must have been made in large numbers in order to make the pottery profitable. There was also competition, for the firm of Doulton & Watts listed 'Hunting Jugs' and 'Figured Tobacco Jars' amongst its products as early as 1818 and by 1873 were advertising tobacco jars from 8d. (about 4p) for the smallest size. Hunting jugs must also have been cheap; for example, the 1829 sales ledger of the London retailers Messrs Thomas Goode lists '1 Hunting Jug & cementing on silver top, 2/6', '3, half pint Hunting Jugs, 4/6', '1 Quart Hunting jug, 2/-' and '1 Hunting jug, 4/6'. The price paid by the retailer to the makers would, of course, have been considerably less. The 1873 illustrated price lists of Messrs Doulton & Watts

Plate 53. *Three hunting jugs. Left, with frieze of 'The Meet', the mount hallmarked 1806 (ex Hill Collection). Middle, with plaque of 'Cock on a Dunghill'. Right, with lunette plaque of 'Cupids' Procession', identical to another example with mount hallmarked 1817. Probably all* **Kishere** *factory, about 1800-10.*

Plate 54. *Tobacco pot, with the 'Punch Party'. Marked* **'KISHERE MOATLAKE'**. *About 1800-10. H. 6¾in. (17.2cm).*   Ex-Hill Collection

and James Stiff list hunting jugs at 3s.6d. (about 17p) per dozen for the smallest size.

There is no evidence that the Kishere pottery benefited from the closure of its rival in 1823. As by this time competition from major producers in London and Derbyshire would have been growing at a great pace, we may imagine that the Kishere pottery managed to keep afloat only by employing some of its family members. Their days of innovation were past so that now they could only follow their bigger rivals. A limited production of bottles must have been necessary, although the tiny amount of £5.19s.4d. duty charged in the 1834 *Report on Stone Bottles and Sweets* indicates that the pottery was in no way able to compete with Wisker at Vauxhall (the owner of the old Sanders pottery) who paid £239.2s.6d., or the growing factory of Doulton & Watts at £38.16s.9d., or more especially the Derbyshire firm of Joseph Bourne which paid £1,020.15s.0d. John Eustace Anderson's *A Short Account of the Mortlake Potteries* in 1894 listed two marked 'half-gallon jars' amongst his own collection, impressed 'W. Brock White Hart Inn' (at Barnes) and 'W. Richards Prince Blucher Twickenham'. These bottles have since disappeared and as no marked Kishere bottles seem to be known to

Plate 55. *Set of graduated face-jugs, some marked* **'KISHERE'**. *About 1820-30.*   Private Collection

the keen modern bottle-collecting fraternity, we must assume that they were either wrongly listed as marked specimens, or extremely rare examples.

The Kisheres did, however, attempt to make other types of ware, as the handful of marked pieces testify. These include a spittoon with a band of foliage marked 'Kishere Pottery Mortlake Surry', a small dish with the same mark, perhaps the base for a plant pot (both at Mortlake Church), a child's mug impressed 'JOHN 1840' at Mortlake Church, a mug impressed 'F. WINCH 1837' and two pieces impressed 'T. HUMPHREY 1842', a colander in a private collection and a chamber pot at the Museum of London with Toby and hunting figures sprigged in the interior – apparently without any symbolic significance, unlike those early nineteenth century chamber pots containing portraits or miniature busts of Napoleon. A marked foot-warmer in John Eustace Anderson's collection, described as round and flat, 8¼in. (21cm) wide with bunches of grapes on each side, has disappeared. An oddity amongst the moulds at Mortlake Church indicates a limited production of gin flasks, formed in this case as a sailor leaning on his anchor (Appendix 9 – D17). A similar mould was used in making a flask at Brighton Museum impressed 'J UNDERWOOD GRAPES 356 ROTHERHITHE WALL' (Plate 66). Since the tenancy of J. Underwood at the Grapes public house was about 1836-47, there is no reason to doubt that this flask type was a Kishere product and most probably one of a number of different types for which the moulds have not survived.

Finally, there are the globular jugs with the pinch-modelled faces on the belly and rims formed as cocked hats; a graduated set of five is marked 'Kishere' (Plate 55). Perhaps intended as measures for a public house, these may possibly be the simpler cousins of a larger and cruder face-jug inscribed 'Vulcan his father kick him out of Heaven because he was so ugly', and on the base 'Mr and Mrs SIVEPSON. Jan 3ʳᵈ 1822' (Christie's 17.5.1976, Lot 90). These pots may relate to a pair of Bristol-glazed ginger beer bottles which were acquired by the Victoria & Albert Museum in 1939 with a verbal provenance back to the son or grandson of an employee of the Kishere pottery – no doubt the 'FA' whose initials are scratched on the base of one of them. They were then stated to represent an Englishman and a Frenchman, though it must be said that neither country would be pleased to claim them as compatriots. If these bottles were indeed the type of utilitarian object made by the Kisheres in the 1830s-40s, as well as perhaps the half-gallon spirit bottles mentioned earlier, it would help to explain both the small but significant bottle tax paid in 1834 and the continuing survival of the pottery, which was forced to close not by economic necessity but by the premature death of its owner. The puzzling feature of these bottles is the Bristol glazing which had been developed by Anthony Amatt at Powell's Bristol pottery in 1835 and which was not manufactured in London for several decades. It was, however, not patented but produced in bulk by J. & J. White at Baptist Mills, Bristol, in order to supply other stoneware potteries, notably those in London where it was not until later in the nineteenth century that a similar (but even less attractive) liquid glaze was developed. There is evidence that when Alfred Singer bought the Vauxhall pottery in 1835 he already had the secret of making the new liquid Bristol glaze, communicated to him by his friend William Powell of Bristol. If the Vauxhall pottery was using Bristol glazing so soon after its invention, there is no reason why the Kishere pottery should not have dabbled with it before its final closure in 1843.

The achievements of the Mortlake potteries were considerable. They brought new shapes to the range of domestic brown stonewares in the late eighteenth century and added self-consciously 'retro' and rustic decoration which ran counter to the smooth creamwares, cheap banded 'Mocha Wares' and the highly refined white porcellanous stoneware beer jugs and mugs mass-produced in the Midlands from about 1800. The appeal of Mortlake wares, with their smooth, almost white clay, reddish freckled iron dip, elegant but sturdy potting, practical handling qualities and range of attractive sprigged motifs in bold relief has never faded – a point proved by Dr. Hugh Diamond presenting a marked tobacco jar to the Museum of Practical Geology in 1875 and the South Kensington Museum (now the V&A) acquiring its first Mortlake tankard in 1878. Despite the small size of the two potteries, the combination of highly attractive product and location near the Thames ensured that the pots became known as far as the heartland of pottery-making, Staffordshire. By way of illustration, a battered Sanders-type baluster hunting jug with a 'Punch Party' plaque was sent by the Burslem manufacturer and pioneer ceramic historian Enoch Wood to Dresden in 1835 (No. 60 on Wood's list, now re-numbered 37488), as a good example of 'Crouch Ware', or English brown stoneware.

It is one of those minor ironies of ceramic history that when the major firms such as Doulton and Stiff developed and mass-produced their own jugs at their vast Lambeth potteries, these soon became just the type of slick, lack-lustre industrial product that had stimulated the potters at Mortlake to invent the original rustic hunting jug nearly a hundred years before. Salt glazing, which offers the advantage of a single-firing, a tight-fitting vapour glaze and opportunities for random colour effects in the kiln, has since enjoyed periods of re-discovery – firstly the idiosyncratic art wares of the Martin Brothers and others in the late nineteenth century, then the oriental-inspired art wares produced at Doultons in the early twentieth century, and more recently the muscular and stylish pots of Mick Casson, Jane Hamlyn and Walter Keeler. Beside any of these, the honest, unpretentious stonewares of Mortlake may still hold their own.

Chapter Five

THE KISHERE FAMILY

A number of historians have speculated on the origins of the Kishere family, including the foremost authority John Eustace Anderson. When writing in the early years of the 1890s,[1] he quoted a generally held belief that Benjamin Kishere's ancestors were Dutch or German Jews. Another author, C. Marshall Rose,[2] asked the question 'Was there any family connection between the tapestry works which flourished in Mortlake in the seventeenth century and the making of Dutch pottery in the village a century later?'

Dealing initially with Anderson's comments, whilst Kishere's ancestors may have been Jewish there is no doubt that Benjamin (1), the head of the Mortlake family, had embraced the Christian faith. Between 1760 and 1776 at least six of his children were christened within the Church of England. The likelihood of a follower of Judaism renouncing his religion is doubtful and the balance of probability must point to a Protestant background.

With religious considerations still in mind, Protestant Holland has to be the favoured choice for the Kishere's country of origin and the introduction of delftware manufacturing to this country could have been the reason for their immigration. Delftware is made from a rough porous clay covered with an opaque glaze obtained by using white oxide of tin. The production technique was perfected in the Dutch town of Delft and at its zenith in c.1680 there were thirty factories employing 2,000 workers from a total town population of 24,000. J.F. Blacker[3] was adamant in stating that 'Lambeth and all other English delft owed its origin to the Dutch. Of that there is no doubt, for the potters who made that ware at Lambeth came from Holland, and many dated pieces are earlier than van Hamme's patent[4] of 1676. But there appears to be no record of the advent of salt-glazed stoneware from the Continent to England'. Apparently there is some merit in the proposition that the first Kisheres to settle in England were skilled delftware potters who emigrated from Holland in the mid-seventeenth century, Germany being an unlikely alternative as their country of origin.

Turning to the question posed by C. Marshall Rose, he speculates on the idea of a family connection between the seventeenth century tapestry workers and the eighteenth century potters of Mortlake. The tapestry works were unique in enjoying not only Royal patronage but also financial assistance from the Crown in establishing the factory and subsidising production as and when necessary. James I initiated the venture in 1619 making a grant of £2,000 to Sir Francis Crane who acquired land on the east side of

Plate 56. *'The North View of Mortlake Church', a drawing by Jean Baptiste Claude (1710?-1771) and engraved by J. Roberts c.1750. Benjamin (1) and Susanna (2) Kishere were married here in 1759. This church of St. Mary the Virgin was the focal point of their religious life where many of their children, grandchildren and great-grandchildren were christened, married, and in the fullness of time buried. The drawing illustrates the north face of the church and to the right is the Queen's Head alehouse with its sign hanging over the centre of the highway.*

Queen's Head Passage and built Tapestry House. The business had a chequered history, on the one hand achieving artistic excellence (Rubens and van Dyck were commissioned to produce designs) and on the other hand a sequence of cash crises indicating that it was not a financial success. Production came to an end in the closing years of the seventeenth century.

A skilled workforce familiar with the art of tapestry weaving was not available in this country and had to be enticed from Flanders. By November 1620 it was estimated that at least fifty Dutch immigrants were employed in the factory and the Mortlake parish records for the ensuing years reflect this influx of foreign workers.

The contrast in skills between the creation of tapestries and the manufacture of delftware is so great as to make any relationship between the Mortlake weavers and the Mortlake potters most improbable. At best we can use the well-documented example of the 1620 settlers as a precedent for supporting the unconfirmed arrival of Delft potters from the mid-seventeenth century, which may have been a more gradual build-up of skilled personnel as existing London potters turned their attention to the production of delftware.

The starting point for the Kishere family tree is Benjamin Kishere (1) who, as we have seen, was employed in the Mortlake pottery of Sanders and probably also in Lambeth where he was doubtless following a family tradition. With some reservations, the writings of John Eustace Anderson provide a helpful, if not entirely accurate, basis from which to trace the subsequent genealogy of the Kishere name. Anderson created one major

The Kishere Family Tree

Family Tree Reference Index Numbers	Reference Pages in the Main Text
(1) Benjamin	84
(2) Susanna née Clarke	85
(3) Samuel	85
(4) Benjamin	85
(5) Jane née Pool	85
(6) Charles	89
(7) Elizabeth	89
(8) Joseph	89
(9) Ann née Griffin	90
(10) Sarah	99
(11) Rachael	99
(12) Jane Elizabeth	86
(13) Benjamin	86
(14) Sarah	86
(15) Elizabeth	86
(16) Thomas	86
(17) Mary	87
(18) Jane	87
(19) Emma	88
(20) Rachael	88
(21) Ann	88
(22) Lucy	89
(23) Charles	89
(24) Margaret Caroline	90
(25) Mary Ann	90
(26) William	90
(27) Mary Ann née Slann	92
(28) Eliza	94
(29) Susannah Ann	94
(30) Anna	94
(31) Frances	95
(32) Ellen	96
(33) John Griffin	96
(34) Jane née Fletcher	97
(35) William John Slann	92
(36) Mary Ann Eliza	92
(37) Zelina Matilda	93
(38) Henrietta Emily	93
(39) Zillah Louisa	94
(40) Frederick	94
(41) Caroline	98
(42) John	98
(43) Joseph	98
(44) Alice	98
(45) William	98
(46) Jane	99
(47) Thomas Squire	88
(48) Arthur Squire	88

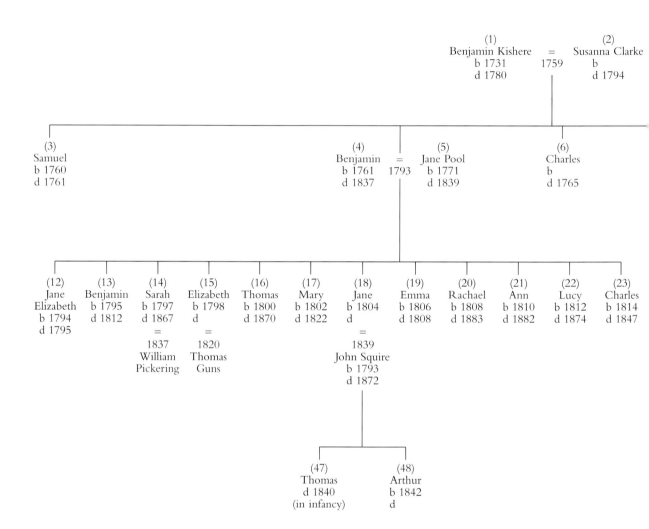

(1)
Benjamin Kishere   =   Susanna Clarke
b 1731   1759   b
d 1780   d 1794

(3)
Samuel
b 1760
d 1761

(4)
Benjamin   =   Jane Pool
b 1761   1793 b 1771
d 1837   d 1839

(5)
Jane Pool
b 1771
d 1839

(6)
Charles
b
d 1765

(12)
Jane
Elizabeth
b 1794
d 1795

(13)
Benjamin
b 1795
d 1812

(14)
Sarah
b 1797
d 1867
=
1837
William
Pickering

(15)
Elizabeth
b 1798
d
=
1820
Thomas
Guns

(16)
Thomas
b 1800
d 1870

(17)
Mary
b 1802
d 1822

(18)
Jane
b 1804
d
=
1839
John Squire
b 1793
d 1872

(19)
Emma
b 1806
d 1808

(20)
Rachael
b 1808
d 1883

(21)
Ann
b 1810
d 1882

(22)
Lucy
b 1812
d 1874

(23)
Charles
b 1814
d 1847

(47)
Thomas
d 1840
(in infancy)

(48)
Arthur
b 1842
d

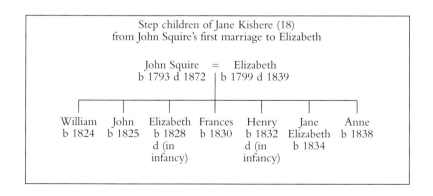

Step children of Jane Kishere (18)
from John Squire's first marriage to Elizabeth

John Squire   =   Elizabeth
b 1793 d 1872 | b 1799 d 1839

William
b 1824

John
b 1825

Elizabeth
b 1828
d (in
infancy)

Frances
b 1830

Henry
b 1832
d (in
infancy)

Jane
Elizabeth
b 1834

Anne
b 1838

MILY TREE

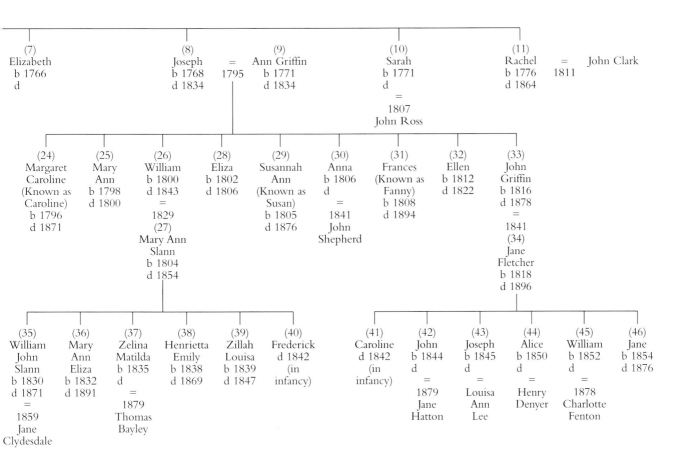

problem which remains unresolved despite much intensive research. He tells us[1] that John Griffin Kishere (33) died on 26 November 1878 and 'His widow Mrs. Lucy Kishere, is still alive, and lives in one of the Sleigh's Almshouses. She has about half-a-dozen specimens of jugs of the Kishere pottery, which are to go to her children on her death'. This may have been written a year or two before 1894, the date of publication of Anderson's work. John Griffin Kishere married Jane Fletcher (34) in 1841, not Lucy, and we can assume that a confused Anderson was referring to Jane. She was certainly alive in 1894, dying two years later, and may well have decided to bequeath her collection of Kishere pottery to her surviving children.

BENJAMIN KISHERE (1) Born 1731 Died 1780

The first Mortlake Kishere mentioned by Anderson (Appendix 7) is Benjamin and our historian states that in 1759 he was one of the leading hands at Sanders' pottery although he does not clarify the significance, if any, of that particular year. An explanation is offered in the preceding chapter and the year becomes even more momentous on examining the Mortlake parish records where we find that 'Benjamin Kishere of the Parish of Mortlake and Susanna Clarke of the same Parish' were married on 23 June 1759. The two witnesses included a John Vernon who had married Mary Clarke on 20 February 1757. Earlier it was suggested that John Vernon worked with John Sanders in the Sanders and Vernon partnership and, having acted as a witness at Benjamin's marriage, it is also evident that John Vernon was a close friend if not a brother-in-law of Benjamin Kishere.

Of the surviving Poor Rate Books (Appendix 1), that for 21 July 1760 has the following entry:

Will'm Walker – Kershaw   [£ Rent] 4   [Rate] 6/-

and an entry in the subsequent Poor Rate Book under the date 29 January 1761 reads:

Wm Walker
ditto   for Kissher   [£ Rent] 4   [Rate] 4/-

Kershaw and Kissher are understandable mistakes and must refer to Kishere. The two entries appear to indicate that William Walker had a legal interest in the property, paying the Poor Rates etc., and Benjamin Kishere occupied the house as a tenant. There are innumerable breaks in the sequence of Rate Books and the next available record relates to 2 October 1772:

Benja Kishere   [£ Rent] 4   [Rate] 4/-

The omission of Wm. Walker's name must have some significance but, as the Poor Rate was levied on inhabitants and occupiers of lands and tenements etc. within the said parish of Mortlake, it is impossible to draw any firm conclusions as to the actual ownership of the property.

As mentioned in the previous chapter a slight doubt surrounds Benjamin's date of birth which assumes that the baptism at St. Mary's Church, Lambeth on 27 June 1731 was of this gentleman. However, the year of his death is incontrovertible, the date of burial being documented as 3 September 1780. Unfortunately Anderson was mistaken in believing that Benjamin Senior was an Overseer of the Poor in 1802 and this reference must relate to his son Benjamin (4).

SUSANNA KISHERE (née CLARKE) (2) Died 1794

Anderson spells her given name with a final letter 'H' but this is inconsistent with numerous entries in the Mortlake parish records, including her marriage and the christening records of her children. During the marriage to Benjamin, Susanna is thought to have given birth to seven children, three girls and four boys, two boys dying in infancy.

The death of her husband at the early age of forty-nine must have left Susanna with considerable financial problems. Her eldest son Benjamin, then nineteen years old, may just have completed his apprenticeship as a builder and could have been making a modest contribution to the family budget. Joseph, only twelve years of age, shortly to be apprenticed to John Sanders, and his two sisters, aged eight and four years, would not have been wage earners. Susanna's difficulties are immediately reflected in the Poor Rate Assessment of 4 September 1780, only days after her husband's death, in which the name of Mrs. Kishere is annotated as 'poor' and no rate is levied. The records for 21 March 1793, twelve months before her death, show no apparent improvement in the financial situation.

SAMUEL KISHERE (3) Born 1760 Died 1761

Samuel is believed to be the first born of Benjamin and Susanna but sadly he died in infancy. He was christened on 27 June 1760 and buried only six months later on 11(?) January 1761.

BENJAMIN KISHERE (4) Born 1761 Died 1837

He was christened on 10 July 1761 and in the 1770s served an apprenticeship with a Hammersmith builder, subsequently starting his own business in Mortlake. Although he may have undertaken general building work, he appears to have specialised in carpentry since a reference to this trade appears in Pigot's 1826/7 Directory.

Benjamin and his younger brother Joseph are reported by Anderson to have won a prize in the State Lottery and Benjamin may have used his windfall towards the starting-up costs of his carpenter's shop in the High Street. Between 1804 and 1837 the Court Rolls include at least eleven references to Benjamin Kishere, recording his attendance as a copyholder at the meetings of the Wimbledon Manorial Court which included Mortlake. In the Survey of 1811 (Appendix 2) we can see that he owned (possibly jointly) three rented houses with a rateable value of £5 each, qualifying him as a copyholder. From the same survey it is apparent that he rented or leased his house, carpenter's shop, yard and shed from John Sanders. By 1811 or earlier Benjamin had achieved some status in the local community.

Having reached the age of seventy-six he died on 1 April 1837. Benjamin married Jane Pool, a local girl.

JANE KISHERE (née POOL) (5) Born 1771 Died 1839

A Thomas Poole appears regularly in the Poor Rate books from April 1773 onwards and, whilst there is a minor variation in the spelling of the name, he was no doubt Thomas Pool, the Mortlake baker referred to by Anderson. His daughter Jane, named after her mother, was christened on 3 January 1772 and buried at the age of sixty-seven on 12 March 1839. Jane Pool married Benjamin Kishere in 1793 and between 1794 and 1814, a period of twenty-one years, they produced no fewer than nine daughters and three sons.

JANE ELIZABETH KISHERE (12) Born 1794 Died 1795

Benjamin and Jane's first child, Jane Elizabeth, survived for only seven months, dying on 25 March 1795 and not 1793 as noted in the Mortlake Churchyard Records. She was christened on 21 September 1794.

BENJAMIN KISHERE (13) Born 1795 Died 1812

The next child of this marriage, a son, was given his father's name and worked with him in the building and carpentry business. Unfortunately his life was brief and he died on 29 June 1812 at the age of only sixteen. The baptism records read: 'Benjamin, son of Benjamin and Jane Kishere, christened 2 August 1795'.

SARAH KISHERE (14) Born 1797 Died 1867

Sarah was the eldest surviving daughter of Benjamin and Jane, having been christened on 26 February 1797. Anderson makes a brief reference to her life – 'She married Mr. Pickering, a butler, who died leaving her a widow with no children. She subsequently lived with her sister Mrs. Jane Squire' (18). Sarah's marriage to William Pickering was solemnised at the Old Church, St. Pancras on 7 September 1837 (City of Westminster Archives). Two years later William's name appears as witness to the marriage of his sister-in-law Jane Squire. Sarah's death is noted in the Cemetery Records as 21 December 1867, age seventy.

ELIZABETH KISHERE (15) Born 1798

In addition to the record of her baptism – 'Elizabeth, daughter of Benjamin and Jane Kishere, christened 12 October 1798' – the International Genealogical Index includes a reference to the marriage of Elizabeth Kishere to Thomas Guns in the Mortlake Parish Church on 25 September 1820. The name of Thomas Guns recurs as a witness to the marriage of his sister-in-law Jane (18) in 1839.

THOMAS KISHERE (16) Born 1800 Died 1870

Using Anderson as the source, we learn that 'Thomas enlisted as a soldier and became an army pensioner, dying unmarried after his father's death, and he was buried at Ealing'. The phrase 'dying unmarried after his father's death' gives the impression that Thomas outlived his father by only a few years although there is some possible evidence to the contrary.

His year of birth is confirmed by the baptism records which show his date of christening as 17 August 1800. The index of deaths at the General Register Office for the quarter to December 1870 contains an entry relating to a Thomas Kishere, age seventy, such entry emanating from the Brentford Register Office. Residence in Ealing could account for the registration of this death in nearby Brentford and if this entry does refer to the Mortlake family then Thomas died some thirty-three years after the death of his father (4) who was buried in 1837.

MARY KISHERE (17) Born 1802 Died 1822

Mary's death at the early age of twenty undoubtedly accounts for the lack of information about her, apart from the official records. She was christened on 6 October 1802, daughter of Benjamin and Jane Kishere, died on 20 October 1822 and was buried on 1 November following.

JANE KISHERE (18) Born 1804

Only three of Benjamin and Jane's twelve children married: Sarah (14), Elizabeth (15) and Jane. Jane's marriage was solemnised on 14 November 1839 at St. Mary's Church in the parish of Mortlake when she was thirty-five years old, having been christened on 23 November 1804. The marriage certificate describes her husband as John Squire, a widower, employed as a parish clerk and the son of Francis Squire, a carpenter. John Squire's first wife, Elizabeth, died some seven months earlier on 27 April 1839, aged thirty-nine. Witnesses to the marriage were Thomas Guns and William Pickering, Jane's brothers-in-law, and Lucy Kishere (22) her youngest sister, then aged twenty-seven.

Jane was involved in a business venture with her three younger sisters who are collectively listed in an 1838 Trade Directory as J.R.A. and L. Kishere [Jane, Rachael (20), Ann (21) and Lucy (22)], Straw Bonnet Makers. If we accept the evidence of an 1840 directory, Rachael and Ann had withdrawn from the partnership leaving Jane and Lucy to continue the business and yet, by 1862, Rachael appears to be the sole proprietor: the full entry in the directory for that year reads – 'Rachael Kishere, Straw Bonnet Maker, Sheen Lane, Mortlake'. This is a most unlikely sequence of events after taking into consideration other information and the use of abbreviated titles in the directories.

We can accept that the four sisters were in business together in 1838 and earlier but Jane married John Squire in November 1839, inheriting a family of five children ranging in age from one to fifteen years. Faced with these new responsibilities she must have taken a less active role in the millinery business and probably withdrew from the partnership shortly afterwards. Prior to 1882 it was illegal for a married woman, but not a widow or spinster, to be involved in any trade or business on her own account, whether as sole proprietor or in partnership with others.

The Census Returns then help to continue the story. In 1841 Rachael, Ann and Lucy, but not Jane, are all described as straw bonnet makers and appear to be living and trading from High Street premises of which their youngest brother, Charles (23), is designated as head of the family. Ten years later, in 1851, the address changes to 18 Sheen Lane. The move to new premises may have resulted from the death of Charles in 1847. The 1861 Return repeats the same information. By 1871 Rachael, Ann and Lucy were still living at 18 Sheen Lane although they had ceased trading and all are described as retired milliners. Anderson refers to their residence as 'The Worple Lodge' at the corner of North Worple Way (presumably the junction with Sheen Lane), a property which served as a private home for the three 'Kishere milliners' together with a workshop and a retail establishment with bonnets and hats displayed in the ground floor windows.

To summarise, the four sisters started the millinery business at some date prior to 1838, Jane left the partnership following her marriage in November 1839 and the three unmarried sisters continued trading until retirement between 1861 and 1871. The Trade

Directories are shown to be very misleading.

The Census provides a further understanding of John Squire's family. In the 1851 Return he is described as a schoolmaster, a profession which may have superseded his earlier vocation unless the duties of parish clerk were of a part-time nature. He was born in St. Giles, Devon and there were five surviving children of his first marriage to Elizabeth; a son Henry and a daughter Elizabeth died in infancy. In 1851 the children are listed as:

John	age 25	Undergraduate at London University
Frances	age 21	School mistress
Jane Elizabeth	age 16	
Anne	age 12	Scholar at home

The eldest son William, christened on 21 March 1824, is not mentioned in the 1851 Mortlake Census Return.

The second marriage to Jane Kishere added two children to the family, although in 1851 only one was alive:

Thomas (47) died in infancy and was buried on 9 September 1840

Arthur (48), christened on 29 September 1842, lived abroad.

John Squire died in 1872, aged seventy-nine, and was buried on 14 June. Jane Squire was still alive when Anderson wrote his book, published in 1894, and must then have been in her late eighties.

EMMA KISHERE (19) Born 1806 Died 1808

Emma's brief life can be counted in months rather than years. Her baptism appears in the parish records under the date of 12 December 1806 and she died on 25 September 1808.

RACHAEL KISHERE (20) Born 1808 Died 1883

Rachael's involvement with her three sisters in the millinery business is recounted above and, despite the inclusion of her name in the 1871 Trade Directory, it is realistic to accept her own affirmation of retirement as quoted in the Census Return for that year. This indicates that the venture was wound up towards the end of the 1860s, certainly between 1861 and 1871, and by that time Rachael would have been in her early sixties having been christened on 13 May 1808. Subsequently she probably left Mortlake and moved to Camberwell. That supposition is based on information from the General Register Office showing that her death was reported to the Camberwell District Office and she was buried in that parish on 16 October 1883, aged seventy-five.

ANN KISHERE (21) Born 1810 Died 1882

Ann, the third sister in the millinery partnership, was christened on 28 February 1810, daughter of Benjamin and Jane Kishere. She lived to the age of seventy-two and was buried on 16 September 1882.

LUCY KISHERE (22) Born 1812 Died 1874

Lucy was the youngest daughter of Benjamin and Jane Kishere and the fourth sister to work in the millinery enterprise. Parish records give the date of her christening as 15 July 1812 and burial on 5 December 1874. She died on 27 November 1874, aged sixty-two.

CHARLES KISHERE (23) Born 1814 Died 1847

The earliest record of Charles, the youngest son of Benjamin and Jane Kishere, is his baptism on 27 April 1814. After completing his education we can surmise that he served his apprenticeship, either by indenture or less formally with his father, learning the trades of building and carpentry. Benjamin died on 1 April 1837 and his son Charles, then aged twenty-three, was ready to take over the business which operated from premises in Mortlake High Street. His name appears in an 1838 Trade Directory where he is described as a builder, and again in 1840, but on this occasion he is listed as a carpenter. He enjoyed the status of master builder for just ten years, dying unmarried at the age of only thirty-three on 26 December 1847.

CHARLES KISHERE (6) Died 1765

Dennis Kishere, a direct descendant of the Mortlake Kisheres, is now living in Australia and undertook some research into his family history. His papers include a reference to Charles, a son of Benjamin and Susanna, who was baptised on 2 September 1765 and buried less than nine months later on 15 May 1766. The source of this information is not stated and the dates conflict with a transcript of the Mortlake parish records, available at the Surrey History Centre, which quotes his date of interment as 15 May 1765, not 1766. It also follows that the suggested date of his baptism cannot be correct. The revised burial date equates more readily with the christening of Elizabeth Kishere (7) as the original information left a gap of only five months between her baptism and that of Charles.

ELIZABETH KISHERE (7) Born 1766

Benjamin and Susanna's first daughter was given the name of Elizabeth at her christening on 31 January 1766. The event is listed in the Mortlake parish records but nothing further is known of her life.

JOSEPH KISHERE (8) Born 1768 Died 1834

Joseph, the youngest son of Benjamin and Susanna, was the founder of the Kishere Pottery. Parish records show that he was christened on 30 June 1768 and buried, aged sixty-six, on 29 December 1834. Anderson provides a little background information to add to the basic facts – 'Joseph kept a horse' (perhaps not unusual for a successful businessman when the horse was the only form of land transport), but then states that he attended race meetings, indicating that his interest in horses may have extended beyond their utilitarian purpose. The 1811 Survey (Appendix 2) shows that he rented from F.M. Ommanney, a banker and churchwarden, two acres of land – a useful pasture and modest exercise area for a racehorse. Joseph's involvement with the pottery is dealt with in the main text.

His marriage to Miss Ann Griffin at St. Martin in the Fields appears in the parish records in the City of Westminster Archives and reads :

Joseph Kishere of the Parish of Mortlake in the County of Surrey Bachelor and Ann Griffin of the Parish Spinster were Married in this Church by L.B.L. this Twenty sixth day of April 1795 by me Plaxton Dickinson, Curate.

This marriage was then solemnised between [Signed] Jos Kishere

Ann Griffin

In the presence of [Signed](?) Taylor

Geo. Gairdner (?)

ANN KISHERE (née GRIFFIN) (9) Born 1771 Died 1834

Joseph's wife, Ann, gave birth to nine children between 1796 and 1816. Anderson mentions that she was the daughter of a Westminster poulterer. Her burial is recorded as 5 December 1834, aged sixty-three.

MARGARET CAROLINE KISHERE (known as CAROLINE) (24) Born 1796 Died 1871

The frequency of infant mortality in the eighteenth and nineteenth centuries undoubtedly persuaded parents to have their children baptised within one or two months of birth. Using this argument Caroline's year of birth has been assigned to 1796 on the evidence of her christening on 26 February 1796 but acknowledging that she may have been born in late 1795. She was the first child and eldest daughter of Joseph and Ann Kishere.

Bearing in mind her father's occupation as a master potter, it is not surprising to find Caroline in an associated trade. The available Mortlake Directories list her as the sole proprietor of a China and Glass Warehouse in 1838 and as a China Dealer in 1840 and also 1862; by this latter date she would have been sixty-six years old and must have retired a year or two later.

Another Directory listing has to be mentioned. In 1838 she is named as the joint proprietor with her younger sister, Susan (29), of a Preparatory Day School in Mortlake.

Caroline died a spinster in the fourth quarter of 1871 and her death was registered at the District Office of Wandsworth, in which area she may have lived in the closing years of her life.

MARY ANN KISHERE (25) Born 1798 Died 1800

Mary Ann, daughter of Joseph and Ann Kishere, died shortly after her second birthday. Parish records give the date of christening as 8 June 1798 and her burial as 16 December 1800.

WILLIAM KISHERE (26) Born 1800 Died 1843

William Kishere succeeded to the Kishere pottery on the death of his father, Joseph, in 1834. William's year of birth is confirmed by the date of baptism of 25 May 1800. Both Anderson and the Churchyard Records are misleading in quoting his age as forty when he died on 22 April 1843, whereas the parish records are correct in quoting his age as forty-three at the date of his interment on 5 May 1843. This latter source is likely to be

Plate 57. *A south-west view of St. Martin in the Fields published by T. Malton on 16 May 1795, the year and church in which Joseph Kishere (8) and Ann Griffin (9) married.* COURTESY OF THE WESTMINSTER CITY ARCHIVES

more reliable than a weathered inscription on an old headstone on which a worn '3' could easily be mistaken for '0'.

William married Miss Mary Ann Slann on 15 June 1829 at St. Bride's Church, Fleet Street, London (City of Westminster Archives).

MARY ANN KISHERE (née SLANN) (27) Born 1804 Died 1854

Once again there is a discrepancy between the various records and, whilst the date of death, 6 April, may be correct, the year is 1854 and not 1853 as stated by Anderson. Her funeral took place on 20 April 1854, when aged fifty, and that year was noted in the Mortlake parish records and confirmed at the General Register Office.

Interestingly the 1851 census gives her occupation as a China and Glass Dealer based in Mortlake High Street. The business is not listed in Pigot's 1840 Commercial Directory and the shop was probably opened at some date after the death of her husband, William, and the sale of the Kishere pottery in late 1844 or early 1845 when capital would have been available for the new venture. She must have been in direct competition with her sister-in-law Caroline (24) who, as explained above, was in a similar business by 1838.

She gave birth to six children.

WILLIAM JOHN SLANN KISHERE (35) Born 1830 Died 1871

It is strange that Anderson omits to mention the eldest son of William and Mary Ann who was given the name of his father. However, young William receives recognition in the 1851 Mortlake Census where he is described as the unmarried son of Mary Ann Kishere, widow. The address is quoted as the High Street and he is said to be living at home, aged twenty years. A similar but less informative entry is to be found in the 1841 Census Return.

Specific information comes from The City of Westminster Archives which show that he was christened William John Slann Kishere on 24 September 1830 at St. Bride's Church, Fleet Street, where his parents were married in the previous year.

Understandably, nothing further was known of this young man until the Dennis Kishere research papers revealed that his great grandfather, William, emigrated to Australia in 1852 where he married Jane Clydesdale on 14 July 1859 and died on 10 December 1871 at the early age of forty-one.

MARY ANN ELIZA KISHERE (36) Born 1832 Died 1891

Mary Ann Eliza was twenty-one years old when her mother, Mary Ann Kishere (27), died in 1854 and we can be reasonably certain that she continued the business started by her mother. This is based on the 1861 Census Return quoting her occupation as 'China and Glass Warehouse' [proprietor]. Further confirmation is provided by the Post Office Directory of Surrey 1862 which includes two Mortlake china dealers, Caroline Kishere (24) and her niece Mary Ann Eliza Kishere. The latter was still trading in 1884, the Directory for that year quoting the business address as the High Street although Anderson locates the china and glass shop as the second house on the east side of Queen's Head Passage.

The formal records are threefold:

1. Mary Ann Eliza, daughter of William and Mary Ann Kishere, christened 25 November 1832.
2. Kishere, Mary Ann E. 58. Richmond S. died in the quarter to March 1891.
3. Mary Ann Eliza Kishere, buried 26 March 1891, 58 yrs., by coroner's order.

This reference to a coroner reveals that an inquest was held to establish the cause of death. According to Anderson's chronicle she was a spinster living alone.

ZELINA MATILDA KISHERE (37) Born 1835

William and Mary Ann were adept at finding unusual and distinctive names for their children, including Zillah and Henrietta. Their third child was no exception, being named Zelina Matilda at her baptism on 20 December 1835; she appears as Zelina in the various Census Returns.

Anderson, however, refers to her as Selina and relates that she married a Mr. B., subsequently 'living in the country'. On the death of her sister Mary Ann Eliza (36), known to be in 1891, Zelina gave Anderson 'about half-a-dozen specimens of family pottery'.

Zelina married late in life, at the age of thirty-nine according to the copy marriage certificate, but if reliance is placed on the parish records, as confirmed by the 1841 and 1851 Census Returns, she must have been forty-three or forty-four years old. The ceremony was held in the Mortlake Parish Church on 6 November 1879 and her husband is named as Thomas Bayley, a widower, aged fifty, living in Walsall and working as a plate glass silverer. Witnesses were Cecil Bernard Slann and Mary Beatrice Slann, relations of Zelina on her mother's side of the family. 'Living in the country' does not readily evoke an image of 'living in Walsall' but we have to assume that Zelina moved to the industrial West Midlands.

HENRIETTA EMILY KISHERE (38) Born 1838 Died 1869

Conflicting information has not helped in finding the correct place for Henrietta in the Kishere family tree and unravelling the puzzle is a challenging exercise. The starting point is the Mortlake cemetery records which state that she died on 3 March 1869, aged twenty-three, and her year of birth would therefore fall in either 1845 or 1846. However, her father, William Kishere (26), died at least twenty months earlier on 22 April 1843 and the cemetery records cannot, therefore, be accurate.

Turning to the General Register Office, her death in the quarter to March 1869 agrees with the cemetery records but quotes her age as twenty-six, not twenty-three. Her year of birth now becomes 1842 or 1843, compatible with her father's date of death.

Unfortunately this simple solution is once more thrown into disarray by the Mortlake Census Returns for 1841, 1851 and 1861 which are summarised below.

1841 Census			1851 Census				1861 Census		
	Age				Age				Age
	M	F			M	F			F
William	35		[Died in 1843]						
Mary		25	Mary Ann	Head		40	[Died in 1854]		
William	10		William	Son	20		[No entry]		
Mary		8	Mary Ann [Eliza]	Daur		18	Mary A.	Head	25
Zelina		7	Zelina	do		16	Zelina	Sister	22
Emily		3	Harriot	do		13	Henrietta E.	do	19
Zillah		1	[Died in 1847]						

The immediate dilemma is to decide whether the Emily of 1841 and the Harriot of 1851 are also the Henrietta E. of 1861. Henrietta was a very common name in the early nineteenth century and became Harriet or Harriot in everyday speech. The age progression from three to thirteen between 1841 and 1851 leads to the conviction that the names Emily and Harriot are synonymous with Henrietta Emily. In 1861 she ought to have been twenty-three – not nineteen – years old and it is impossible to explain why the ages of all three sisters are understated by three or four years.

The significance of the data, if correctly interpreted, is evident: Henrietta Emily was born in 1837 or 1838 and died in 1869, aged thirty-one or thirty-two. However, as we have already seen, this contradicts the official nineteenth century records which to some extent must have been subject to the fallibility of human memory.

ZILLAH LOUISA KISHERE (39) Born 1839 Died 1847

Zillah, a daughter of William and Mary Ann Kishere, died when only eight years of age and was buried on 13 November 1847.

FREDERICK KISHERE (40) Died 1842

The details on the death certificate cover the whole of this very brief life:

> When and where died:- 29th September 1842 at Mortlake, age 4 weeks. Occupation:- Son of William Kishere, potter. Cause of Death:- Thrush.
> Informant:- Lowry Hilsden present at death, Mortlake. [Signed with a cross.]

ELIZA KISHERE (28) Born 1802 Died 1806

This daughter of Joseph and Ann Kishere survived for less than four years. Her christening took place on 3 December 1802 and she was buried on 15 June 1806.

SUSANNAH ANN KISHERE (known as SUSAN) (29)
Born 1805 Died 1876

At the baptism of Susan on 4 July 1805 she was given the forenames of her grandmother and mother. It is said by Anderson that she occasionally helped in the Kishere Pottery owned by her father, Joseph, but her real interest lay in education. Susan is listed in Pigot's 1838 Directory of Surrey as the proprietor of a preparatory day school, understood to have been in Mortlake High Street and, as already mentioned, she was joined at the school by her sister Caroline (24) in or before 1840. In that Caroline had a separate business interest, the partnership with Susan may have been a financial rather than a working relationship.

Susan's death at the age of seventy-one was registered in the last quarter of 1876 in the Wandsworth Registration District which may not have any special significance. She is reported by Anderson to have died at Priest Bridge, Mortlake and whilst Richmond Register Office would have been marginally nearer, Wandsworth was only three miles to the east.

ANNA KISHERE (30) Born 1806

Of Joseph and Ann's seven daughters, four reached maturity and only one, Anna, was to marry. The wedding was celebrated on 15 July 1841 some thirty-four years after her christening on 5 November 1806. Her youngest sister, Frances (31), appears as one of the witnesses. The bridegroom, John Shepherd, was a butler and Anna joined him in working for the same employer.

Plate 58. *St. Bride's, Fleet Street. 1753. Engraving by Donswell. William John Slann Kishere (35) was christened in 1830 at St. Bride's where his parents, William Kishere (26) and Mary Ann Slann (27), were married in the previous year.*

The property to the left of the engraving with the angled corner joining the west and north walls is situated on the junction of Salisbury Court and Fleet Street. It is No.82, the Fleet Street premises occupied between c.1780 and 1809 by Andrew Abbott, the well-known London china dealer, and his various partners. In 1817 fire destroyed the property which was rebuilt and leased to Davenport in the following year. A specific reference to the unsafe 'West Front Corner' wall appears in a demolition order served by the City of London in June 1817. The draft of an advertisement written at some date between 1784 and 1787 states that Turner and Abbott stocked 'a matchless variety of Hunting Jugs and Mugs some mounted with Silver'. COURTESY OF THE GUILDHALL LIBRARY, CORPORATION OF LONDON

FRANCES KISHERE (known as FANNY) (31) Born 1808 Died 1894

Anderson names Fanny as a daughter of Joseph and the writer's only comment is that she lived in London, a fact confirmed by other records. Her death at the age of eighty-five was reported to the Lambeth Registrar and, unusually, there is a note that she died in Kennington. The Cemetery Records give her date of death as 20 April 1894 and her interment as Tooting.

She probably spent the first thirty or forty years of her life in Mortlake. At the date of the June 1841 Census, Fanny, then aged thirty-two and incorrectly quoted as twenty, was living in the High Street with her sisters Caroline (24) and Susan (29) and her brother John (33). She is described as a school mistress and could have been teaching at Susan's preparatory school. Her name is not included in the 1851 Mortlake Census implying that she had moved to London by this date.

Frances was christened on 11 November 1808, the daughter of Joseph and Ann Kishere.

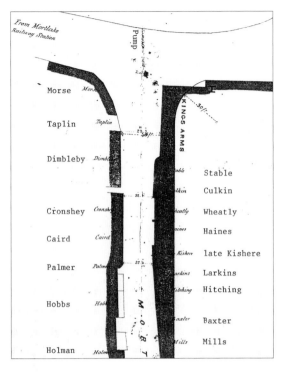

Plate 59. A detail from the 'brewery map' of March 1865 which, by coincidence, names the occupiers of the properties in the High Street photograph (Plate 60) taken at about the same date. On the north side of the High Street the reference to 'late Kishere' almost certainly relates to John Griffin Kishere (33) and his family who were living at No. 8 High Street, Mortlake at the time of the Census returns in 1851 and 1861, although they had moved to Victoria Terrace by 1871. Evidently the property was empty when the map was prepared in 1865, the Kisheres having vacated the house shortly before that date. The name Wheatly appears on the map and is associated with No. 3 High Street in the Census returns, helping to confirm the allocation of low house numbers to the western end of the High Street.
COURTESY OF THE LOCAL STUDIES LIBRARY,
RICHMOND UPON THAMES

ELLEN KISHERE (32) Born 1812 Died 1822

The youngest daughter of Joseph and Ann lived for only ten years. Ellen was baptised on 2 September 1812 and buried on 21 August 1822.

JOHN GRIFFIN KISHERE (33) Born 1816 Died 1878

John was the youngest child and second son of Joseph and Ann. He did not share in the good fortune of his elder brother William (26) who inherited the Kishere Pottery. In the 1841 Census Return he was living in the High Street with his sisters Caroline (24), Susan (29) and Frances (31), and is described as a carter. John was 'brought up to the pottery business', to quote Anderson, and he could have worked alongside his father, Joseph, for some six years prior to the latter's death in 1834. This may have prompted John to seek an alternative trade outside the family, in preference to working for his brother.

At the time of his marriage in July 1841 he describes himself as a brewer and his employment at the Mortlake brewery, part owned by a Mr. Topham, is mentioned by Anderson. John was a 'brewer's servant' in 1854 when his daughter Jane (46) was baptised, and a 'drayman' at the time of the 1861 Census, presumably still working for the Mortlake brewery. If so he had seen a number of changes in the brewery's ownership – there were no less than eight different firms during the nineteenth century of which Topham featured in two, viz. Halford and Topham and Topham and Kempson. His progression from carter to drayman and then to undertaker, as described in the 1871 Census, has a certain logic if we visualise John Kishere driving a horse-drawn hearse.

John and his wife Jane parented six children, their first born, Caroline (41), dying in infancy. His own death came on 26 November 1878 at the age of sixty-two.

Plate 60. *A view of Mortlake High Street looking east and photographed from The Green in c.1865.*
COURTESY OF THE LOCAL STUDIES LIBRARY, RICHMOND UPON THAMES

JANE KISHERE (née Fletcher) (34) Born 1818 Died 1896

Little was known of Jane, John's wife, apart from her date of death, 8 November 1896 at the age of seventy-eight, and her place of birth which is quoted as Oxfordshire in the 1851 Census Return and as Kingston in the 1861 Census. A search of the *Oxfordshire Gazetteer* does not reveal a town or village with the place name of Kingston but there are two neighbouring hamlets located five miles south-east of Thame using Kingston as a prefix, namely Kingston Blount and Kingston Stert. The files in the General Register Office indicate that a branch of the Kishere family lived in that area of Oxfordshire; the marriage of another John Kishere in 1866 and the death in 1879 of an Arabella Kishere aged thirty-two were registered in Thame.

A copy of John Griffin Kishere's marriage certificate helps to complete the picture:

12th July 1841. Marriage solemnised in the Church of Aston Bewant.

John Kishere, Brewer, Mortlake. Father's Name Joseph Kishere dec'd.

Jane Fletcher, Servant, Aston. Father's Name Thomas Fletcher, Labourer.

In all probability John Griffin Kishere met his future bride, Jane Fletcher, when visiting relatives in the vicinity of Thame. Aston Bewant, where they were married, is within a mile or two of Kingston Blount and Kingston Stert and there is little doubt that Jane was born in one of those two Kingstons and either her family moved to Aston Bewant or, alternatively, at the time of her marriage she was a servant residing with her employer in that hamlet.

CAROLINE KISHERE (41) Died 1842 (in infancy)

John and Jane's first child lived for only a few months. Caroline was born in the quarter to September 1842, christened on 4 November 1842 and buried on 30 November in that year.

JOHN KISHERE (42) Born 1844

The 1861 Census describes John as the seventeen year old, unmarried son of John and Jane Kishere and his employment as a merchant's clerk. He was born in the first quarter of 1844, probably January, and given his father's name at his baptism on 18 February 1844. He married Jane Hatton in 1879.

JOSEPH KISHERE (43) Born 1845

Joseph, the second son of John and Jane, was christened on 22 September 1845. At the time of the Census in April 1861 he was fifteen years of age and employed as an apprentice carpenter. There are two other references to a Joseph Kishere which could be germane to him. Firstly, the name appears in Kelly's 1899 *Directory of Surrey* under the heading of Private Residents which quotes 29 Tremerne Road as his address. Trehern Road is likely to be the present-day equivalent of Tremerne Road. Secondly, the marriage of a Joseph Kishere was advised to the Brentford Register Office in the quarter to December 1864 and, if the reference is applicable, he was then only nineteen years old.

Further details of this marriage are to be found in the City of Westminster Archives which quote the bride's name as Louisa Ann Lee, the date as 1 November 1864 and the parish as Isleworth.

ALICE KISHERE (44) Born 1850

Alice was a ten year old scholar, according to the April 1861 Census Return, and that age is verified by the date of baptism which took place on 24 November 1850. She was the daughter of John and Jane Kishere and married Henry Denyer.

WILLIAM KISHERE (45) Born 1852

Christened on 25 April 1852, William, the son of John and Jane Kishere, is listed as a scholar, aged nine, in the 1861 Census and at the age of nineteen the subsequent return gives his occupation as a pawnbroker. We must conclude that he was employed by a pawnbroker rather than having the necessary capital to conduct his own business.

On 4 May 1878 he married Charlotte Fenton, aged twenty-eight, a resident of Mortlake and the daughter of George Fenton, an iron-worker. The copy marriage certificate cites William's occupation as a coachman and his brother Joseph (43) and sister Alice (44) as witnesses.

JANE KISHERE (46) Born 1854 Died 1876

The basic facts of Jane's brief life are well documented and, whilst she is mentioned by Anderson in his book *Rambles of Old Waram,* he gives us no background information. The General Register Office places Jane's date of birth in the first quarter of 1854 and the parish records state that she was baptised on 26 February 1854, daughter of John and Jane Kishere, Mortlake, brewer's servant. The cemetery records note that she died on 25 November 1876 in her twenty-third year and, turning again to the parish records, that she was buried on 3 December 1876, aged twenty-two years.

SARAH KISHERE (10) Born 1771

Benjamin (1) and Susanna's (2) fifth child was christened Sarah on 15 September 1771 according to the Mortlake parish records. The next reference to a Sarah Kishere is to be found in the International Genealogical Index (I.G.I.) which lists the marriage of a lady of this name to John Ross on 24 February 1807 in the district of Marylebone. Sarah's pedigree as a Mortlake Kishere is proven, but the marriage details are less certain.

RACHEL KISHERE (11) Born 1776 Died 1864

There are many references to this lady, the youngest child of Benjamin (1) and Susanna (2). She was baptised on 10 February 1776 (Mortlake parish records) and married John Clarke (or Clark) on 12 March 1811 at St. Anne's Church, Soho (I.G.I.). The 1841 Census Return includes a Rachael Clark, of independent means, living with Caroline Kishere (24) and her two sisters (Appendix 3). She is again listed in 1851 as Caroline's aunt, a widow aged seventy-three. She died on 4 February 1864 aged eighty-eight as recorded in the Mortlake Cemetery Records.

Mortlake in the
County of Surrey to Wit.

A Rate or Assessment
made this 29 day of January 1761 on
the Inhabitants and Occupiers of Houses
Lands and Tenements &c. within the said
Parish of Mortlake in the County
aforesaid for and towards the necessary
Relief of the Poor of the said Parish for
one half year Comencing from Michael
1760 to Lady day 1761 by the Church
Wardens and Overseers of the said Parish
and with the consent of Two of his Majesties
Justices of the Peace for the said County
(of whom One is of the Quorum) according
to the Statute in that case made and
provided ————————————

RATE BOOKS

The Mortlake Rate Books are available at the Local Studies Room in the Richmond upon Thames Library. They are handwritten notebooks detailing assessments and the collection of rates for the Relief of the Poor, for Maintenance of the Highways, for Upkeep of the Church and so on. The earliest is dated 6 June 1754 and they continue for well over a hundred years. Unfortunately they are of limited use as many of the earlier books are missing, so giving rise to major breaks in the chronological sequence, and they usually only quote the name, the rent [rateable value?] and the amount of the assessment. The sparsity of addresses leads to uncertainty in drawing a coherent picture of events and there is seldom a distinction between commercial and residential use of property. Specimen pages from the Poor Rate Assessment of 29 January 1761, which are clearly written and include an early reference to Benjamin Kishere, are illustrated in this appendix.

The more significant entries in the Rate Books relevant to the Kishere story have been selected and are referred to either in the main text or by separate notes at the end of the appendix.

	£ Rent	Assessment
6 June 1754		
Mr. Will'm Sanders	21	1. 1s. 0d.
21 July 1760		
Will'm Walker – Kershaw	4	6s. 0d.
29 January 1761		
Wm Walker)		
do for Kissher)	4	4s. 0d
2 October 1772		
Benja Kishere	4	4s. 0d.
Jn Vernon	6	6s. 0d.
1 April 1773		
Thos. Poole	5	5s. 0d.
23 September 1776		
Mr. Wm Sanders	25	1. 5s. 0d.
Benja Kishere	4	3s. 0d.
Mr. Jona Sanders – From end June £12 only	20	7s. 6d.

	£ Rent	Assessment
14 March 1780		
Mr. Kishere	4	4s. 0d.
4 September 1780		
Mrs. Kishere	4	-
16 March 1784		
Mr. W. Sanders	25	1. 17s. 6d.
do Dwelling House	31	2. 6s. 6d.
11 September 1784		
Mr. Wm. Sanders	25	1. 17s. 6d.
do Dwelling House	31	2. 6s. 6d.
March 1786		
Mr. J. Sanders & Co	25	1. 11s. 3d.
do Dwelling	31	1. 18s. 9d.
Mr. Prior House & Malthouse	37	2. 6s. 3d.
14 March 1791		
Works £25 Messrs. Sanders & Co)		
Dwelling House, Fields etc.)	-	4. 6s. 0d.
John Prior House and Malthouse	37	-
22 September 1791		
Widow Kishere	Poor	-
26 March 1793		
Widow Kishere	-	-
Benja Kishere	11	5s. 6d.
24 November 1794		
John Vernon	12	-
22 September 1795		
Mr. John Sanders	31	-
Joseph Kishere	12	-
September 1797 (Poor Rate Book)		
East Sheen Lane		
Joseph Kishere Emp	12	-
November 1797 (Surveyors' Rate Book)		
East Sheen Lane		
Joseph Kishere Paid for potters	10-12	6s. 0d.
28 September 1798		
Joseph Kishere	10	13s. 4d.
1810/1811 Mortlake Surveyors' Collecting Book		
Mr. Benja Kishere	12	
do Land Mr. Biggs	2	7s. 0d.
Mr. Jos. Kishere 2 Ten'ts	18	
do Land Mr. Ommanneys	3	12s. 0d.
Mr. B. Kishere	11	7s. 0d.
22 September 1812		
Mr. Benja Kishere	17	
do Garden	2	
do Shed	4	1. 8s. 9d.
Mr. Joseph Kishere	24	
do Tenem't Warehouse	6	
do Land of Mr. Ommanneys	3	2. 1s. 3d.

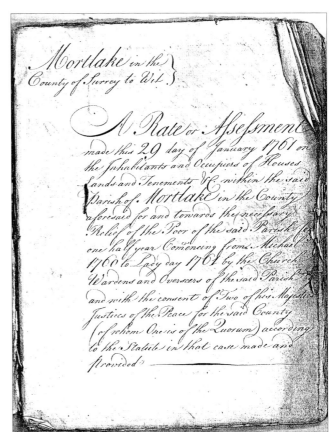

Plate 61. *Specimen pages from the Poor Rate Assessment of 29 January 1761 including entries for William Sanders and 'Kissher'. William Sanders also signed the document as an 'inhabitant'.*

Edw.d Langley .... £ — 5 ✗
D.o for Land late Funnells ..... — 1 ✗
Jo.s Middleton .... — 5 ✗
Late Sears Emp. Blank .... — —
    Fairbank Poor .... — —
James Du Pree .... — 6 ✗
Henry Ellcock .... — 1 ✗✗
George Bourn .... — 3 ✗✗
Will.m Ansell .... — 5 ✗
The Rev.d M.r Arnold ... — 6 ✗
Doct. Simpson .... 1 14 ✗
Eliza. Jones .... — 15 ✗
M.r Will.m Sanders ..... 1 1 ✗
John Hemm .... — 5 ✗
Late James Yarner Emp ..
Edw.d Fisher Poor .....
James Drown .... — 6
Sarah Boddicott Poor ...
                2   £ 6 . 12 —

Henry Cook .... £ — 2 ✗
Will.m Jackson .... — 4 ✗
M.r Lamy .... — 15 ✗
Christ.r Hammatt ......
Late James Terry Emp ...
Sarah Vinegar Poor .....
Wid.o Snelling .... — 4 ✗
John Pulley .... — 5 ✗
    Reed no Cert now Pol.s Earls
Wid.o Walton Poor .....
Rich.d Watson Sen.t Poor ...
Rich.d Watson Jun.t Poor ...
W.m Walker .... } — 4 ✗
D.o for — Kissher ... }
W.m Barnett .... — 10 ✗
Wid.o Vernon Poor .....
M.rs Marth.a Taylor ... — 8 ✗
John Roberts .... — 4 —
                10   £ 2 . 16 —

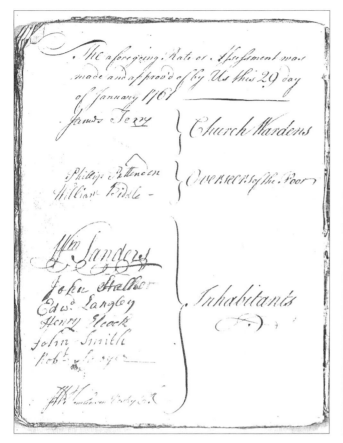
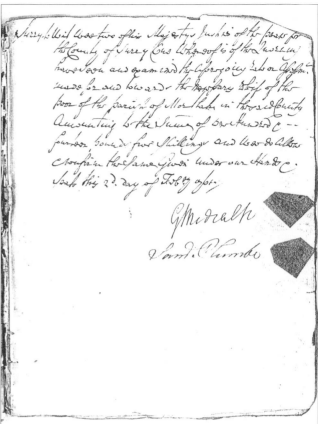

William Sanders

William Sanders' name appears in the first available Poor Rate Book of June 1754 and continues in subsequent assessments until September 1784. The 'rent' of £21, rising to £25, relates to the pottery which also included a house, probably occupied by the Sanders family, as evidenced by the March 1784 entry when a separate dwelling house, 'rent' £31, is added. A few years earlier, in September 1780 and again in June 1782, he was assessed for a property with a 'rent' of £11 which may be the dwelling house re-assessed at £31 after major building works or refurbishment.

John Sanders

William Sanders died on 29 September 1784 and his son, John, continued the business, subsequently taking a Mr. Vernon as a partner. These changes in the ownership of the pottery are reflected in the March 1786 entry when '& Co' is added to the name of J. Sanders.

Mr. Jona Sanders' name can be traced back to September 1775 and linked with a 'rent' of only £3 but in the following year he is shown as occupying a substantial property with a 'rental value' of £20.

A John Vernon is to be found in the records as early as October 1772 and the name recurs, albeit erratically, until 1798. He could be a strong candidate for John Sanders' partner, Mr. Vernon.

⌐ Appendix 2 ⌐

SURVEY OF 1811

A handwritten copy of the survey is held in the Local Studies Room at the Richmond upon Thames Library. The preamble and relevant references to the Kisheres read as follows:

A
Survey and Estimate
of the
Lands and Tenements
in the Parish of Mortlake
in the
County of Surrey

———————

Surveyed pursuant to an order of the Commissioners
for carrying into execution the Acts of Parliament
for granting to His Majesty a contribution on the
profits arising from property, professions, trades
and offices.

Dated the 13th of April 1811

Proprietors	Occupiers	Description	Value	Observations
John Sanders	Richard Palin [Cooper]	House Sheds Work-shop and Yard	18	Relieved on appeal to £15
do	James Quick [Butcher]	House Slaughter House and Stables	18	
John Sanders	Benjamin Kishere [Carpenter]	House Carpenters Shop Yard and Shed	20	Relieved on appeal to £17
John Biggs	do	Land	2	0.0.30 acres

Proprietors	Occupiers	Description	Value	Observations
David Seal	Joseph Kishere [Potter]	House Pottery Stables Shed & Yard	24	
F.M. Ommanney	do	Land	3	0.2.0 acres
David Seal	do	Tenement and Wharehouse [sic]	6	
John Sanders	John Wisker [Potter]	House Pottery and Yard	120	Relieved on appeal to £112
Benj'm Kishere *R. Pettiward*	Benjamin Kishere [Carpenter]	Shed	4	
do	William Huntingdon [Coal Merchant?]	House	5	Rent £5
do	James Boxall	do	5	
do	Richard Collyer	do	5	Rent £7
John Sanders	William Pembroke	House Offices and Gardens	55	
Roger Pettiward	James B. Phillips [Coal Merchant]	Coal Warehouse	19	
George Fournier	William Watson [Whitesmith]	House Smiths Shop Yard and Garden	21	

Note

The items shown in parentheses are entered on the handwritten copy in red ink by the Borough Librarian who was attempting to identify the trades of the occupiers of the listed properties. However, the insertion of R. Pettiward alongside the name of Benjamin Kishere in the proprietor's column is impossible to explain with any certainty. If the author of the Survey was rectifying an earlier omission then we have to assume that the first of the properties, and possibly all four, were jointly owned by the two parties.

CENSUS RETURNS
(Examined 1841 to 1871)

Despite some shortcomings the Census Returns are a useful supplement to the Churchyard, Cemetery and Parish Records in researching the genealogy of the Kisheres. Those for Mortlake are held in the Local Studies Room at the Richmond upon Thames Library.

The 1841 and 1851 Enumerators Returns are photocopies bound in volumes and the 1861 and 1871 listings are held on microfilm. The original 1841 documents have deteriorated over the years and many of the photocopies are extremely difficult to read. Street names are included but unfortunately there are no house numbers; perhaps this was of little importance prior to the introduction of the penny post by Sir Rowland Hill in 1840 and only gradually became essential as the service gained in popularity. It should also be noted that in the 1841 Returns the ages for adults are rounded to the nearest five years. Subsequent Returns improve in clarity and detail.

A specimen page from the 1851 Census Return is illustrated in this appendix and references to the Kishere family are listed below.

<u>June 1841 Census Return</u>

High St	William Kishere	35	Potter
	Mary "	25	
	William "	10	
	Mary "	8	
	Zelina "	7	
	Emily "	3	
	Zillah "	1	
High St	Charles Kishere	25	Carpenter
	Lucy "	25	Straw Bonnet Maker
	Ann "	25	"
	Rachael "	30	"
High St	Caroline Kishere	40	Dealer in China
	Susan "	25	School Mistress
	Frances "	20	"
	John "	20	Carter
	Rachael Clark	60	Independent Means

<u>1851 Census Return</u>

High St	John Squire	Head	Mar	58	School Master	Devon/St. Giles
	Jane "	Wife	Mar	46		Mortlake
	John "	Son	Un	25	Under Graduate [sic] at London University	"
						"
	Frances "	Daur	Un	21	School Mistress	"
	Jane Elz" "	Daur	Un	16		"
	Anne "	Daur		12	Scholar at Home	"
	Arthur "	Son	–	8	do	"
High St	Caroline Kishere	Head	Un	54	Dealer in China & Glass	
						Mortlake
	Susanna Ann "	Sister	Un	44	School Mistress	"
	Rachael Clark "	Aunt	Wid	73	Annuitant	"
High St	John Kishere	Head	Mar	34	Brewer's Lab	"
	Jane "	Wife	Mar	32		Oxfordshire
	John "	Son		7	Scholar	Mortlake
	Joseph "	Son		5	do	"
	Alice "	Daur		3 mths		"
High St	Mary Ann Kishere	Head	[Wid]	48	China & Glass Dealer	Middlesex London [?]
	William "	Son	U	20	At Home	Mortlake
	Mary Ann "	Daur	U	18	do	"
	Zelina "	do	U	16	do	"
	Harriot "	do	U	13	do	"
Sheen Lane						
	Rachel Kishere	Head	U	42	Straw Bonnet Maker	"
	Ann "	Sister	U	40	do	"
	Lucy "	do	U	38	do	"

*(**Opposite**) **Plate 62.** Specimen page from the 1851 Census Return listing Caroline Kishere, her sister and aunt as residents of 24 High Street, Mortlake.*

345

Parish or Township of	Ecclesiastical District of	City or Borough of	Town of	Village of

6

No. of House	Name of Street, Place, or Road, and Name or No. of House	Name and Surname of each Person who abode in the house, on the Night of the 30th March, 1851	Relation to Head of Family	Condition	Age of (Males / Females)	Rank, Profession, or Occupation	Where Born	Whether Blind, or Deaf-and-Dumb
						Total of Persons.... 8 10		

1861 Census Return

High St	John Squire	Head	Mar	68	Collector of Rates	Devon/ St. Giles
	Jane "	Wife	Mar	56		Mortlake
	Ann "	Daur	Un	22		"
	Arthur "	Son	Un	18		"
High St	Caroline Kishere	Head	Un	60	China Dealer	"
	Susan "	Sister	Un	49	"	"
High St	John Kishere	Head	Mar	45	Drayman	Mortlake
	Jane "	Wife	Mar	42		Kingston
	John "	Son	Un	17	Merchs Cl.	Mortlake
	Joseph Kishere	Son		15	Carpenter (Ap)	"
	Alice "	Daur		10	Scholar	"
	William "	Son		9	do	"
	Jane "	Daur		7	do	"
High St	Mary A. Kishere	Head	Un	25	China & Glass Warehouse	"
	Zelina M. "	Sister	Un	22		"
	Henrietta E. "	Sister	Un	19		"
East Sheen						
	Rachel Kishere	Head	Un	52	Straw Bonnet Maker	"
	Anne "	Sister	Un	51	do	"
	Lucy "	do	Un	48	do	"

1871 Census Return

6 Victoria Terrace	John Kishere	Head	Mar	55	Undertaker	"
	Jane "	Wife	Mar	52	None	Oxon. Kingston
	William "	Son	Unm	19	Pawnbroker	Mortlake
Sheen Lane	Rachel Kishere	Head	Unm	62	Retired Milliner	"
	Ann "	Sister	Unm	61	do do	"
	Lucy "	Sister	Unm	58	do do	"
17 High St	Eliza Kishere	Head	Unm	39	Dealer in China & Glass	"
	Zelina "	Sister	Unm	37	do	"
High St.	John Squire	Head	Mar	78	Annuitant	Devon Torrington
	Jane "	Wife	do	66	None	Mortlake
	Ann "	Daur	Unm	33	Teacher	"

THE BROOK WATSON 'BROADSIDE'

A transcript of a printed pamphlet, signed anonymously and circulated or brought to the attention of liverymen of the City of London. The original is in the Guildhall library where it is appropriately described as a 'broadside'.

To the worthy Liverymen of the City of London.

Gentlemen.

I am astonished to see, in a paper of this day, the very extraordinary address of Mr. Brook Watson to you, soliciting your suffrages to represent you in Parliament; wherein he says, *Unconnected with, and uninfluenced by any man, or set of men, permit me to solicit your interest and support on this occasion.*

To try this assertion by the standard of truth, I beg leave to ask the following questions:-

1. Is he not a native of America?

2. Did he, or did he not, exert his best endeavours to support that most wanton, accursed, cruel and ruinous war against his countrymen?

3. Did he, or did he not, receive emoluments and contracts in Lord North's administration, to facilitate that unnatural war?

4. Did he, or did he not, accept of the Commissary-Generalship in America, because he should have a pension for life of 365 guineas per annum?

Independent of these emoluments, where is his estate of qualification?

If Mr. Watson can negative these questions, I do admit his address to you stands on fair ground; but if he cannot, he is undeserving of your countenance!

Jan. 16, 1784   A. LIVERYMAN.

Appendix 5

KISHERE IMPRESSED MARKS AND WINDMILL SPRIGS

The known Kishere marks are illustrated in the top row of Plate 63. They are dated to (A) c.1800, (B) c.1810–1830, (C) c.1810–1820 and (D) c.1830–1843.

A number of the windmill sprigs can be attributed to Kishere, others to Sanders' pottery and at least one is common to both potteries.

Type I	Appears on a marked Kishere hunting jug but is also found on wares attributed to Sanders.
Type II	A reliable indication of Kishere origin.
Type III	Probably a Sanders sprig.
Type IV	Probably a Sanders sprig.
Type V	From a mould in the Mortlake Church Collection and attributed to Kishere, dating to c.1830–1843.
Type VI	A reliable indication of Kishere origin dating to c.1830–43.

(Opposite) Plate 63. Kishere impressed marks and windmill sprigs.

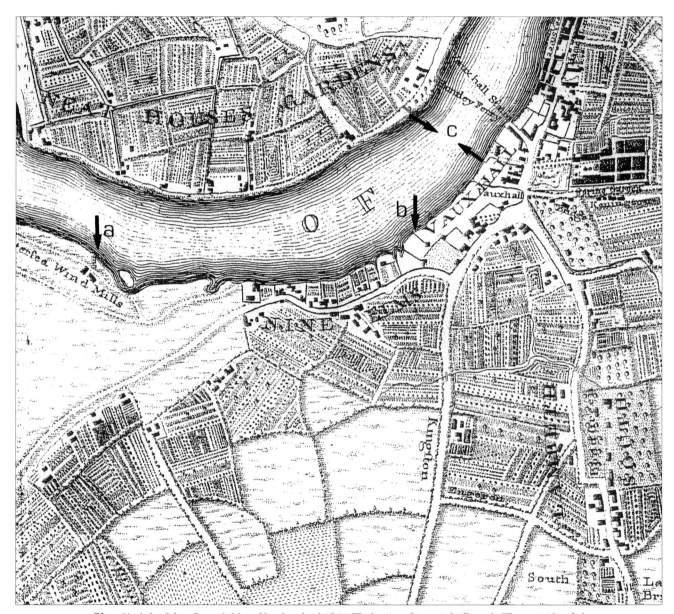

Plate 64. *A detail from Rocque's Map of London, dated 1746. The location of two windmills on the Thames is identified in Frank Britton's* London Delftware[1] *at (a) Battersea and (b) Nine Elms. Their relationship to the future Vauxhall Bridge (c), opened in 1816, helps to authenticate the supposition that the windmill in the foreground of Plate 13 is the one acquired by Sanders and Crisp in 1753 or earlier.*

THE NINE ELMS WINDMILL

The ownership of the Nine Elms windmill by the Sanders family, John Sanders, his son William Sanders and his grandson John Sanders, can be traced for a period of some ninety years from 1753 and the mill was probably in existence prior to that date. Two sources provide the chronological data: the Hand-in-Hand Insurance Company documents researched by Frank Britton, *London Delftware,* Jonathan Horne 1987 and Michael Short, *Windmills in Lambeth an historical survey,* Director of Library and Amenity Services of the London Borough of Lambeth 1971. Michael Short consistently spells Sanders' name as *Saunders* which is retained when quoting from his book below.

1753	The first reference to the Nine Elms windmill appears in the Battersea rate book showing as owners Sanders & Co, the partnership between John Sanders and Nicholas Crisp which existed from 1751 to 1758.
1755-58	Rated to John Sanders & Co.
1758	John Sanders died, probably leaving the Mortlake potworks to his son William and also an interest in the Lambeth pottery jointly with Henry Richards, William's brother-in-law.
1759-66	Throughout this period the windmill was rated to Henry Richards & Co. (presumably William Sanders and Henry Richards trading as).
1759	The ownership becomes a little confused as the records of the Hand-in-Hand Insurance Company note that Nicholas Crisp and William Sanders insured the Nine Elms windmill. It may have been leased to Henry Richards & Co.
1762	The site of the windmill appears on Rocque's map of this date.
1763	Nicholas Crisp was declared bankrupt.
1780	The Land Tax books attribute the ownership to William Saunders and a leasehold interest to Randall & Co.
1781-99	With the exception of one year, probably a mistake, the Land Tax books record Saunders as the proprietor.
1784	William Sanders died, his estate passing to John Sanders, his son.
1802	The change of ownership is reflected in the Land Tax entry recording John Saunders as proprietor.
1835-38	The Rate book entries show the owner as Saunders and occupier Charles Knott.
1839-42	The Rate books continue to show Saunders as the proprietor but the mill is then occupied by Messrs. Francis & Co.
1840	John Sanders died.
1843	Ownership passed to the South Western Railway Company and the windmill was demolished a few years later.

JOHN EUSTACE ANDERSON

John Eustace Anderson's book, *A Short Account of the Mortlake Potteries,* is an invaluable catalyst for any research into the Kishere family and their involvement with the local potteries. J.F. Blacker, in his *ABC of English Salt-Glaze Stoneware from Dwight to Doulton* (published in 1922), devotes a chapter to 'Mr. Anderson on Mortlake', quoting extensively from his book. More recently Robin Hildyard acknowledged the importance of Anderson's legacy to ceramic historians when compiling his article on 'Mortlake Saltglaze' for the April 1993 issue of *Antique Collecting.*

Anderson's style is simplistic and some of his writing has an endearing naïvety, particularly in the *Rambles of Old Waram,* giving the impression of a gentle, friendly man with a ready sense of humour. He was born in 1843 in Southampton, the son of Lieut. Colonel Eustace Anderson, an attorney-at-law practising in Lincoln's Inn Fields. The family moved to Mortlake in 1854 and John Eustace was educated at King's College where presumably he studied law, joining his father's practice in 1859. He was admitted a solicitor and attorney-at-law at Easter 1865 and subsequently became a partner with his father in the firm of Anderson and Anderson based at a new address in the City at Ironmonger Lane.

He accepted various public duties following the death of his father in 1889 and succeeded him as clerk to the old Highway Board. Four years later the parishes of Barnes and Mortlake were granted local self-government and he was appointed clerk to the Barnes Urban District Council, a post he held until his retirement in 1911 when he became consulting solicitor to the Council.

Apart from his involvement with the law he served with the Victoria Rifles, 1st Middlesex R.V. Corps from 1861 until the early 1890s, retiring with the rank of Major. The Reserve Volunteers were a military force of trained civilians enlisted for use in times of emergency, comparable with the Territorial Army of today.

John Anderson's obituary in the *Richmond Herald* of 2 October 1915 tells us that his health had been failing for some time although he continued his public duties, even attending a meeting of the Mortlake Overseers on the day prior to his sudden death on 26 September 1915, aged seventy-one years.

Surviving records from the last century provide additional information and help to update his *Short Account of the Mortlake Potteries* which remains an important reference point, despite its many shortcomings. For that reason an unabridged copy is appended.

A SHORT ACCOUNT

OF THE

MORTLAKE POTTERIES.

BY

JOHN EUSTACE ANDERSON.

(Printed for Private Circulation.)

Richmond, Surrey:

R.W. SIMPSON, PRINTER, SHEEN ROAD.
1894.

It appears from statements made by different writers that Delft and earthenware were manufactured here in the eighteenth century.

Delft-ware is earthenware covered with white glazing in imitation of porcelain, formerly made at Delft in Holland.

Stoneware is a species of potter's ware of a coarse kind, glazed and baked.

The first pottery for Delft-ware was established by a Mr. William Sanders (said to have been married here on the 25th of March, 1748), between 1742 and 1752 in premises on the north-side of the High-street, by the water side, now known as St. Mary's Wharf, opposite the Church, and which has on its east-side the site of the Old Maltings, now occupied by Samels'-terrace and a boathouse at the rear, forming a portion of the Mortlake Charity Estate, having been left to the parish by Mrs. Joanna Hullenberch in 1662.

I find Mr. Sanders' name in Rate Books from 1754 to 1784, but he may have been rated earlier and later, as the Rate Books are not all in order.

He was succeeded in the business by his son John, who lived in the house known as Ivy House, East Sheen, on the east-side of the corner house and premises occupied at one time by a Mr. Paine, subsequently by Mr. Selmes, and now by Mr. William Dunkley, all carrying on the business of a butcher.

Mr. John Sanders died here, and was buried in our Old Churchyard on the west-side of the Church.

There were two kilns at the pottery, one for white ware and the other for coarser work.

In the first ten or fifteen years of this century Mr. Sanders sold the business to Messrs. Wagstaff and Co., of the Vauxhall Pottery.

A few years afterwards Mr. Wagstaff was succeeded by his nephew, Mr. John Wisker, who, on the 28th May, 1821, made a return under the Census Act that there was one family living in his house, consisting of one male and one female. How this was I do not know, as I understood he lived in London. He might, however, have had a London house besides.

A Mr. John Prior, living in the High-street near the premises, assisted in the business as foreman or manager. There was also a Mr. Gurney, living in the same street, who also held a good position in the works.

About 1827 the whole business was transferred to the Vauxhall Pottery and the works closed. Thus became extinct our first Mortlake Pottery, after having been in existence more than 70 years.

It is stated that "Toby Philpot" jugs were first invented in Mortlake, being manufactured both at Sanders' and Kishere's Potteries. They were brown and of a very common ware.

I have a small one made at Kishere's Pottery. The top rim is made to represent a three-cornered hat, the liquor being poured out at one of the corners, which acts very well as a spout. On the front of the jug, which is round, is formed very coarsely a nose and chin projecting, with scratches to represent the eyes, mouth, and whiskers. These jugs were novelties at the time, but ceased to be so after 1796.

There is at South Kensington Museum a large punch bowl of Delft ware, made, I believe, at Sanders' Mortlake Pottery about 1780. It is enamelled earthenware, blue, with scrolls on a white ground, with figures of birds, masks, medallions, and flowers. It is over 20 inches in diameter, and over a foot in height.

Also twelve tiles of Delft, painted in dark blue on a white ground, representing a rocky landscape, with ruins and figures, about 19in. by 14in.

It is stated that they were presented by Mr. Alfred Stringer.

I have in my possession a watch stand (which was presented to me), made by Gurney, the potter in Wisker's employ about 70 years ago, and given by him to the late Miss Rachel Kishere. It is 5½ inches in height, by 3½ inches wide and 1½ inches in depth. It is on a white enamelled ground, with a scolloped blue-lined edge front and back.

On the front is a church with a spire, and house with three trees. There is a hole for the face of the watch, and underneath is a man with a fishing rod, with a woman and two trees by some water, and a fence. The sides are ornamented in blue square patterns.

In 1888 Mr. Thomas Goddard, a very old inhabitant, who lived at 1 Industry-place, at the old school end of Mullin's-path, showed me about a dozen articles of plates, &c., very coarsely made, in white with a number of small red flowers on them, made at Wisker's Pottery. He also said he had a few cups and saucers.

Specimens of the above kind of Delft ware seem to be very uncommon in Mortlake itself, for saving the above mentioned specimens, I have never come across any others in the place, or heard of their existence.

In addition to the pottery on the north side of the High-street, there was one on the south side, which was started some years after the other, but lasted about twenty years longer.

The origin of this second pottery was as follows:—

In 1759 one of the leading hands at Sanders' Pottery was a Benjamin Kishere. I find his name in the rate book of 1774, and as overseer in 1802.

It is supposed that his ancestors were Dutch or German Jews, "Kishere" being a corruption probably of the name "Kish."

One of the family, an ancient woman, amused me once by reciting a few verses on the subject of her own composition. The first portion related to finding out the origin of names, and that in searching the Scriptures she found the name of Kish, a man of Benjamin. The last verse, as far as I can remember, was as follows:—

>This best of names I will now tell,
>My friends do pray give ear,
>My friends did give an "ere" of course,
>And turned it into Kish*ere*.

This Benjamin Kishere had two sons by his wife Susannah, one named Joseph, who was an apprentice at Sanders' Pottery, and the other Benjamin, who was apprenticed to a builder at Hammersmith.

Joseph married a Miss Griffin, a poulterer's daughter, of Westminster, and by her had a little money, which, together with a prize which both he and his brother Benjamin obtained in a State lottery, gave them a start in life.

Joseph built a pottery on the south side of the High-street, where Mr. Pether and Mr. Eydman's shops stand at the present time, with Martha's place at the back, and commenced business on his own account, manufacturing, it is said, white stone ware; but this, I think, must be wrong. as I have only seen brown ware, and a person whose memory goes back 80 years cannot recollect anything but brown ware being manufactured at this pottery.

He appears to have been a man fond of horses, and kept one. He also attended race meetings, not a very lucrative branch, I should say, of a potter's business, although sometimes we hear of a man making a "pot" of money, whatever that expression may mean.

I find his name down in the rate book in 1810, and ascertained by a parish record that he collected the poor rate in 1813, and in October, 1833, was the Surveyor of Highways.

Sir Richard Phillips, in his walk to Kew in 1817, describes how in going through the High-street, Mortlake, westwards from the Church, he turned aside to view a manufactory of Delft and stone-ware, for which among potters Mortlake was then famous. He says a silly air of mystery veiled these workshops from public view, and as he professed his to be a visit of mere curiosity, the conductor's taciturnity increased with the variety of his unsatisfied questions. It was in vain he assured him that he was no potter, that experimental philosophy and chemistry had stript empiricism of its garb, and that no secret worth preserving could long be kept in a manufactory which employed a dozen workmen at 20s. a week. Phillips, as a stranger to Kishere, must have been very innocent if he thought he would have let him into the secrets and mysteries of his trade. Sir Richard goes on to observe that the principal articles made were those brown stone jugs, of which the song told him, "One was made of the clay of Toby Philpot," and he could not help remarking that the groups on the jugs were precisely those on the common pottery of the Romans. The patterns used on the jugs were copied from those used at Delft, of which this manufactory was a successful imitation in every particular. Hunting scenes were depicted on the several vessels: a stag followed by ferocious quadrupeds and hungry bipeds formed their general ornament. He said he had picked up the same groups among Roman ruins, had often contemplated them in the cabinets of the curious, and here he was amused at viewing them in creations but a week old.

Joseph Kishere had two sons, William Kishere and John Griffin Kishere, both brought up to the pottery business, and four daughters, Caroline, who died a spinster in 1871; Ann, married to a Mr. Shepherd, who was butler at Miss Aynscombe's, Old Cromwell House, she also having been in the same service; Susan, who helped sometimes to stamp out the hunting figures in clay and place them on the jugs, and who subsequently kept a school in the High-street, and died at Priest Bridge; and Fanny, who lived in London.

When Joseph Kishere died his son William became possessed of the pottery, and carried on the business with the assistance of a man named John Pollard, whom he employed. The brother, John Griffin, worked for Mr. Topham, the brewer, at Mortlake, for some years, and lived in a small house near the Tithe Barn for about 23 years, dying on the 26th November, 1878, aged 63. His widow, Mrs. Lucy Kishere, is still alive, and lives in one of the Sleigh's Almshouses. She has about half-a-dozen specimens of jugs of the Kishere pottery which are to go to her children on her death.

William married Miss Mary Ann Slann, and had three daughters, Eliza, who of late years lived by herself, keeping a china and glass shop, being the second house on the east-side of Queen's Head-passage, and who died suddenly about two years ago; Henrietta, who died a spinster; and Selina, who married and lives in the country.

It was on the death of Miss Eliza Kishere that her sister Selina (Mrs. B.) very kindly allowed me to have about half-a-dozen specimens of the family pottery.

I have altogether four jugs and two mugs of the Kishere pottery, some stamped at bottom with "Kishere Mortlake Pottery, Surrey." One is a brown jug holding 3½ pints. The upper half is dark brown, the lower part light brown. On the upper part, raised, is the representation of a windmill and a cottage adjoining, with a figure leaning on the half door of the cottage, looking at a woman leading up a donkey with a sack on its back, a small windmill by itself, two trees separate, and two men together, one sitting on a barrel, drinking, and the other sitting, leaning on a table, on which stands a jug. On the lower part of the jug are two horsemen with eight dogs hunting what looks like a fox: it appears two [sic] small for a deer. The other two jugs are smaller, but very similar in style. I have been informed that one of the members of the family had on all his jugs a cottage with a figure leaning on a half door, with a donkey approaching; whilst another member, to distinguish his manufacture from the other, left out the donkey.

Of the two mugs, a quart and pint, the quart is dark brown one-third down from the top, the remaining two-thirds being light brown, the top part of handle dark, and remainder light brown. Round the top half of the mug appear the following raised subjects: small windmill and tree, stout man sitting on bench with small table next him, on which is a glass into which he is pouring something, in the other hand he holds a pipe. On each side of this figure are two raised trees. Adjoining handle is another figure of a man sitting on a cask at a table, with a tree at his back. On the lower part two huntsmen following six hounds in batches of three each, with a fox in front.

An article with a wreath of acorns round it in low relief, intended for the floor of a bar parlour.

Ten years ago there were also two specimens of Mortlake pottery in the Jermyn-street

Museum of drab stone ware, representing hunting and other scenes in low relief. One of them bearing the name of "Kishere, Mortlake," impressed.

Other wares bear the marks "Kishere's Pottery, Mortlake, Surrey." The pottery is represented to be of fair quality, but of no artistic value.

Kishere stoneware is very scarce now in the place. I only know of about five persons in the parish who own from one up to six or seven pieces. Dr. George Rodman has some few pieces which he exhibited recently at the Imperial Institute.

William Kishere died on the 22nd April, 1843, rather suddenly, aged 40. He was buried in a grave midway between the old churchyard railings and the ivy-covered arch on the left hand side of the path leading thereto.

According to the rate book of the 20th July, 1843, his executrix (and widow), Mrs. Mary Ann Kishere, was rated for the house and pottery at £45 gross, and £32 rateable. Her name also appears in the rate book in respect of the same property in October, 1844.

About this time the property was to be disposed of, which, reaching the ears of Mr. John Abbott, of Richmond, china and glass warehouseman, he was desirous of purchasing the place for his son Thomas, who knew something about pottery manufacture.

The result was that the pottery was purchased by his brother, Mr. Thomas Abbott (who subsequently lived and died at Cambridge Lodge, St. Leonards, Mortlake); he let it to his brother, John, at a low rent (whose name appears in rate book as occupier in February, 1845), who thereupon put his son, Thomas, into the place to work the pottery.

This young Mr. Thomas did for about two years, manufacturing coarse pottery, such as dishes, drain pipes, &c. One of these large, coarse dishes, manufactured by him or his man named Attley, which is called a Welsh baking dish, and is marked by alternate curved stripes of brown and yellow, of about half-an-inch broad, running from side to side, has been kindly presented to me by Mr. John Hewson Abbott, and added to my collection of Mortlake potteryware.

The pottery did not seem to answer, as young Mr. Thomas's uncle resumed possession of the premises and soon afterwards built three houses on the front portion, one now tenanted by Mr. Eydman, and the other two by Mr. Wm. Pether.

On the back portion, where the kiln was, he built four cottages, calling them Martha's-place, to reach which is a passage from the High-street on the east side of Mr. Pether's shops.

Mrs. Mary Ann Kishere, the widow of Mr. Kishere, died on the 6th April, 1853, and was buried in the same grave with her husband.

Benjamin Kishere (brother of Joseph) was a builder. He married a Miss Pool, a baker's daughter, who lived in the High-street. The Pools were bakers in Mortlake for several generations, one of them, an Isaac Pool, owned a large dog, which wore on its neck a collar with the following words on it, to be read by any other dog whom he might meet with:— "I am Isaac Pool's dog, but whose dog are you?"

Benjamin and his wife had three sons—Benjamin, Thomas, and Charles, and nine daughters—Jane, Eliza, Sarah, Elizabeth, Mary, Jane Emma, Rachel, Ann, and Lucy. Charles, on his father's death, took up his father's business, but died young and unmarried. Thomas enlisted as a soldier, and became an army pensioner. He died unmarried after his father's death. He was buried at Ealing. Benjamin worked in his father's business, but died young and unmarried.

Jane (now living) married Mr. John Squire (the Parish Clerk), and was left a widow with one son, Arthur, now living abroad.

Sarah married Mr. Pickering, a butler, who died, leaving her a widow with no children. She subsequently lived with Mrs. Squire, and died at her house in the High-street.

Rachel, Ann and Lucy carried on business together for some years as milliners at Worple Lodge, a corner house between Sheen-lane and North Worple-way.

I now conclude my account of all I have been able to gather together of interest relating to our old Mortlake Potteries and the Potter's families.

Before, however, I entirely close my narrative of all that relates to kiln manufacture, I wish to mention that at one time, about fifty years ago, Mr Henry Goodale, a builder, in Sheen-lane, used to manufacture bricks on land opposite Cromwell House Field, at the West end, where some clay is to be found.

He also started a lime kiln on his premises in Sheen-lane, recently occupied by Mr. Kennet, the builder. These several ventures, however, were given up after six or seven years' trial.

Recently a fresh trial of kiln work has been made in the parish, with reference to which I feel I ought to say a few words.

On the 24th June, 1893, the Mortlake West-end School-house, situated in the Lower Richmond-road, near its junction with the Kew-road, was let to Messrs. Ruel Bros., being no longer required for the children in the Gas Works district by reason of that part of the parish having become incorporated with the Richmond Borough since the 9th Nov., 1892.

In the month of June, 1894, I paid a visit to these premises, now occupied, excepting a small portion of land on the east-side, by Messrs. Ruel Bros.

The first thing to be noticed on approaching the place from the east-side are some large letters on the side of the old school wall as follows :—

Established 1819,
Ruel Bros.,
Stourbridge,
Fire, Clay, Tile, and Stove Fitting Works.

On arriving at the front of the premises I found the Old School notice board painted out, and Ruel Bros. painted up instead.

From the chirruping that was going on I noticed also that on the top of the roof, where the school-bell still hangs under cover with its clapper now at rest, the sparrows had taken possession of the place as a snug and peaceful spot within which to make their nests.

Along the front of the building is a low open fence with a small gate, and close to this a small notice board, stating "Trespassers will be prosecuted, by order of the Trustees," presumably a relic of the old school days.

No one appeared to be near. I lifted the latch and walked up the west-side of the building to the back, when I at once came on a small kiln, the side open, and two men standing by—one with clay tiles ready to be put in, and the other, whom I ascertained, on addressing, was Mr. John Ruel, receiving and packing them into the kiln on the north-side.

On my introducing myself, he very kindly showed me how he was packing the kiln which had been built under the personal supervision of himself and brother, somewhat different from the care that has to be taken in packing china cups, saucers, &c., which I had seen done at the Worcester works. Midway from the ground was an iron band round the kiln, and above that on the east-side another aperture, through which he packed light articles.

After the packing is completed the holes are closed and plastered up, there being, however, a pipe vent at the top of the cone, and fires lighted, which have to be carefully attended to for about 40 hours, when they are allowed to go out. It then takes about a day and a half to allow the kiln to cool before it is opened.

Whilst talking, the second brother emerged from the building whom I knew and took me inside, where I saw a large quantity of fire-brick appliances for stoves of every description, including the requisites for gas-stove fittings, some of the articles being of very curious shapes.

I was informed that the moulds were made either of wood or plaster of Paris and that the clay used was brought from Stourbridge and that it is the best of its kind that is used for store bricks, &c.

Mr. Ruel informed me that their father and grandfather before them had had to do with kiln work, that their business was originally commenced at Chelsea, where crucibles were manufactured for Government works, &c.

From Chelsea the business was removed to Fulham, and from thence to the Goldhawk-road, Shepherds Bush.

Whilst their grandfather was at the latter place their father, who was a gold and silver refiner in Holborn, London, took over the business, which was managed for him for a time by their uncle.

Some time after that machinery was introduced for the purpose of manufacturing crucibles, against which it was impossible to compete.

He had been brought up in the refining work, but joined with his brother in starting an entirely new branch of business as carried on by them at the present time.

The lease of their Shepherds Bush premises running, out they resolved to make a move and eventually selected their present premises in Mortlake, where they have now been a year at work.

I was taken to an outbuilding where I was shewn what is termed a muffle, an oven-shaped vessel for the purification of gold and silver by means of a cupel (a small cup) made of burnt bones and therefore somewhat porous. Also to where they stored their goods when finished and ready for sale.

Both the Messrs. Ruel live together in a house at the West-end, opposite Cromwell House field.

I was pleased with my visit and wish them every success in their undertaking.

[250 *Copies Printed.*]

JOHN ANDERSON'S STONEWARE COLLECTION

Under the heading of 'Mortlake Memories', John Anderson made regular contributions to the *Richmond Herald* and in the newspaper's issue dated 12 September 1914 he listed his collection of stoneware given to him by members of the Kishere family. Whilst some of the marked pieces may have been Kishere production lines, the unmarked items will have to remain unattributed. They may include Kishere trial pieces, Sanders wares acquired by Joseph or his father, Benjamin, when working at that pottery, or they could be wares from other manufacturers stocked by either Mary Ann Kishere, William's widow, or Caroline Kishere, William's sister, who were both trading as Mortlake china dealers in the mid-nineteenth century.

The list contained the following items all marked 'Kishere Pottery, Mortlake, Surrey':

Two **half-gallon jars,** with the following words impressed: W. Brock, White Hart Inn' (Barnes) and 'W. Richards, Prince Blucher, Twickenham'.

A **spittoon,** 4½in. (11.4cm) deep x 6in. (15.2cm) wide.

A **jug,** 6¾in. (17.2cm) high and 3¼in. (8.3cm) diameter at mouth, several men (one smoking), a fox, six hounds, and two hunters, blowing horns.

A **mug,** 4in. (10.2cm) high, 4in. (10.2cm) in diameter at mouth, two trees, two men sitting (one smoking), a fox, six dogs, two huntsmen with horns.

A **jug,** 5in. (12.7cm) high, 3in. (7.6cm) diameter at the mouth, huntsmen, windmill etc.

A fine light coloured **flower-pot and saucer,** 5½in. (14cm) high by 5in. (12.7cm) diameter, a wreath of leaves round the pot as also on saucer.

A **foot-warmer,** round and flat, 1¾in (4.5cm) high, 8¼in. (21cm) diameter, with two bunches of grapes on each side.

Tobacco jar and cover [No description of the jar].

The list then continues with articles obtained from the Kishere family but not bearing a maker's mark and therefore giving rise to doubts as to their provenance:

A **jug,** 8in. (20.3cm) high, 4in. (10.2cm) across mouth, number of figures, dogs, and three huntsmen.

A **pot** made without a handle, 3¾in (9.5cm) high, 3¼in. (8.3cm) diameter. Stamped on it is 'John, 1840'.★

A round flat **inkpot,** 1¾in. (4.5cm) high, 4½in. (11.4cm) diameter, six holes round the top in which to put pens. On it are impressed the words, 'Thorp, East Sheen, June 16th, 1814'.

A **pint pot,** windmill, trees, two men (one smoking, the other drinking).

A **mug,** 6¾in. (17.2cm) high, 3¾in. (9.5cm) diameter, windmill, trees, fox, dogs and huntsmen.

A **bottle,** 8½in. (21.6cm) high.

A **jug,** 7½in. (19.1cm) high, 3¾in. (9.5cm) diameter at mouth, stag, dogs and huntsmen.

A **large jug,** 8½in. (21.6cm) high, 3¾in. (9.5cm) diameter at mouth, stag, dogs and huntsmen etc.

A very small **candle-holder,** 2in. (5.1cm) high and 2in. (5.1cm) diameter.

A small oblong **ash-tray,** 3in. x 1¾in. (7.6cm x 4.5cm).

An **Uncle Toby jug,** 5½in. (14cm) high x 4¾in (12.1cm) diameter of hat.

A small **Uncle Toby jug,** 2½in. (6.4cm) high x 1¾in. (4.5cm) diameter, handle broken off.

A small **jug,** 3in. x 1½in. (7.6cm x 3.8cm) dogs and huntsmen, handle broken off.

Two white **vases,** handles broken off both, 7½in. (19.1cm) high x 4½in. (11.4cm).

An **Uncle Toby jug,** 4in. (10.2cm) high, diameter of hat at mouth 3½in. (8.9cm).

★The description of this handleless pot matches item A2 in the Mortlake Church Collection, Appendix 9, which bears the Kishere impressed mark Type D illustrated in Appendix 5. Either two similar pots existed or John Anderson has mistakenly listed the item as unmarked, a more likely explanation.

CATALOGUE OF POTTERY IN MORTLAKE PARISH CHURCH

According to the Church catalogue, dated 1958-59, the origin of this pottery collection is unknown, but if the entries summarised below are compared with Appendix 8 it appears likely that some of the pieces formed part of John Anderson's Stoneware Collection.

A1   Mug 4in. (10.2cm) high, marked on base 'Kishere Pottery Mortlake Surry'. Relief designs above: windmill, tree, fat man smoking, tree, man sitting on barrel with drink. Below: fox, two pairs of dogs, two horsemen with hunting horns.

A2   Mug 3¾in. (9.5cm) high, no handle, marked on base as above. Relief design above: windmill tree and fence, fat man drinking and impressed above 'John 1840', tree. Below: fox, four dogs in a group, two horsemen with horns.

A3   Jug 8½in. (21.6cm) high, no mark. Design on upper part: windmill, tree, fat man sitting drinking, tree, two men sitting on barrels, one smoking pipe, and on lower part: fox, six pairs of dogs running, three horsemen with hunting horns. The glazing and designs are similar to A1 and A2 and this jug may have been made at Mortlake. *[It is now considered to be of Lambeth origin rather than Mortlake. c.1840.]*

A4   Jug 8in. (20.3cm) high, no mark. Handle ends in foliage design at lower end, crossed by a strap. Relief design above: man on barrel with mug of beer, tree and fence, fat man drinking, windmill, man sitting on barrel smoking pipe. Below: stag, five pairs of dogs running, one horseman with hunting horn. *[The jug is now confidently attributed to Lambeth with James Stiff, 1846-1913, as the likeliest potter. c.1870.]*

B5   Pot shaped like unspillable inkwell but larger – 3½in. (8.9cm) high and hole in centre 2in. (5.1cm) in diameter. Also small hole in side of vessel. Band of foliage round middle. Marked on base 'Kishere Pottery Mortlake Svrry'. Purpose of this article unknown. *[Believed to be a spittoon.]*

B6   Lid with pot above, with relief of fox and group of four dogs. Glazed brown in colour. May not belong to B5 as it has a flange on the lower surface for which there is no corresponding rim on the pot. No mark.

B7   Small dish 5½in. (14cm) diameter, with relief band of indeterminate foliage round margin like that on B5. Marked on base 'Kishere Pottery Mortlake Svrry'.

B8   Plant pot 5½in. (14cm) high, no mark, but relief band of foliage as on B5 at height of 3in. (7.6cm) from base, so may have been made at Mortlake. *[Possibly made by Kishere.]*

B9   Plant pot, 4⅛in. (11.4cm) high, no mark. Hole in base. Relief of grapes and foliage all round rim, with four bunches of grapes hanging down. Two rings in imitation of handles. Could have been made at Mortlake. *[Now attributed to Kishere c.1830.]*

C10   Vase 7in. (17.8cm) high in whitish saltglaze, marked rather faintly on the rim of base 'Kishere Mortlake'. Relief round bulbous part: two cherubs blowing horn and holding two dogs on leads, alternating with two groups of four cherubs. Below: fox, two pairs of dogs, horseman without hunting horn. Remains of two handles, broken. *[The Kishere mark is impressed in the clay.]*

C11   Vase 7.5in. (19.1cm) high in whitish saltglaze. Relief above: four cherubs, repeated twice. Below: fox, two pairs of dogs, one dog alone, horseman. Unmarked but similar to C10 and may be of Mortlake origin. *[Possibly Kishere.]*

D12   Mould – tree with fence – two identical moulds side by side on the same block of plaster.

D13   Mould – tree without fence – two moulds side by side on the same block.

D14   Mould – man sitting on a barrel, with a mug of beer beside him on the table. Back of mould has marking scratched on it – ? 'ship 1822' or 'Tup 1022'?

D15   Mould – fat man sitting drinking.

D16   Mould – windmill and house next to it, with a figure of a man or woman leading a donkey.

D17   Moulds – two halves which fit together making a mould 9in. (22.9cm) high, showing the front and back of a man. Pieces of mould join by shallow knobs and hollows, and hollows on the base show that there was a third piece to complete the mould. It would have had an opening at the top (through top of the figure's hat) and been used to make some kind of spirit flask. *[A sailor gin flask taken from similar moulds is in the Brighton Museum and Art Gallery.]*

D18   Mould – hollow semi-circular shape 3½in. x 2½in. (8.9cm x 6.4cm) high showing figures of men and horses in relief. For application to vase?

D19   Mould – to make oval plaque, 3½in. (8.9cm) greatest diameter, female figure draped in classical style.

D20   Mould – to make 'projection' 2in. (5.1cm) high, with shallow fluting. Could have made a kind of plinth or a lip for a vessel.

E21   Circular plaque 5½in. (14cm) diameter showing the head and shoulders of an old woman taking snuff. Surface apparently painted.

E22   Oval plaque 5½in. (14cm) greatest diameter, showing a classical head wearing a helmet – ? head of Athene, Greek goddess of war. Not glazed or painted.

F23   Trade Card: Joseph Kishere
                       Brown Stone Manufacturer
                       Mortlake in Surry
                       Late apprentice to Messrs. Sanders and Vernon
                       Potter *[see Plate 47.]*

This has been used as a receipt. Written on the back: 'Received the 13th April 1818 two Crates for Mr. Pathen Lewis, the George Inn, Borough' (signature illegible).

MORTLAKE CHURCH

STONEWARE COLLECTION

Plate 65. *A general view of the collection in the display cabinet at the Mortlake Parish Church. The individual pieces are illustrated on the following pages.*

Plate 65a.

Plate 65b.

A1 (Marked)

A2 (Marked)

A3

A4

B6

B7 (Marked)

B9

B8

B5 (Marked)

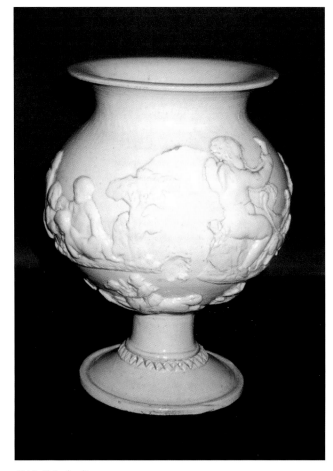

C10 (Marked)

C11

D12

D13

D14

D15

D16

D17

Plate 66. *Spirit flask, moulded as a sailor with anchor, impressed 'J.UNDERWOOD GRAPES 356 ROTHERHITHE WALL' (the landlord's tenancy 1836-47). Made from a larger version of the mould in the Mortlake Church collection (D17). The base is hollow and the fraction on the reverse indicates the flask's half-pint capacity.* **KISHERE factory,** *about 1836-43.* COURTESY OF THE BRIGHTON MUSEUM AND ART GALLERY No.321093

D18

D19

D20

E21

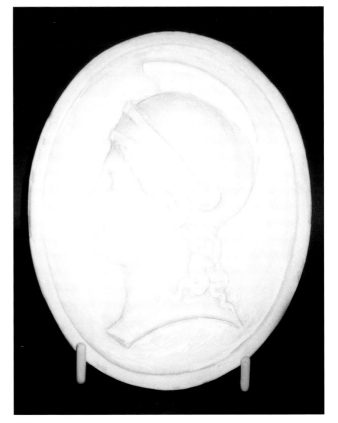

E22

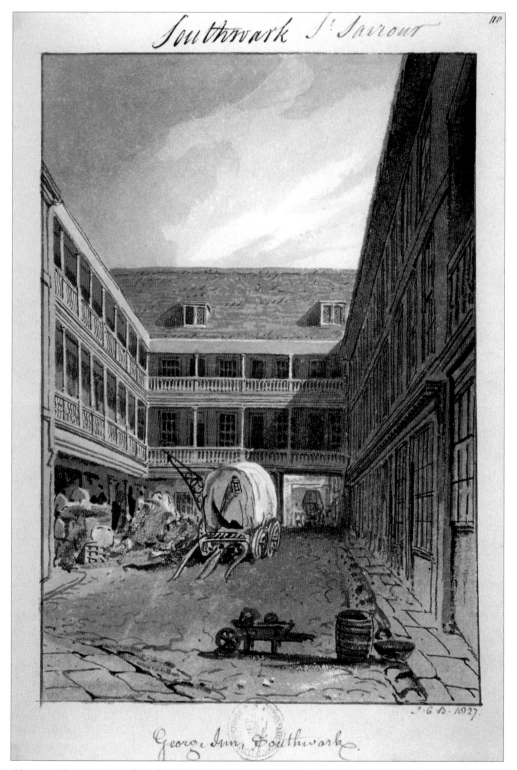

Plate 67. *The reverse side of Joseph Kishere's trade card was used in 1818 to acknowledge a delivery of two crates to the George Inn situated in Borough, a part of Southwark. It is one of the oldest coaching inns in London, first appearing on a map of c.1542 and, following its total destruction by fire in 1676, the inn was rebuilt a year later. The galleried courtyard as it existed in 1827 is well illustrated in the above watercolour by J.C. Buckler.*

COURTESY OF THE GUILDHALL LIBRARY, CORPORATION OF LONDON

THE WILLIAM KISHERE JUG

This remarkable jug is described and illustrated in black and white on page 73. In all probability it was a family memento, dated Nov. 25 1829, relating to an important family event, for example, a Christmas gift from William Kishere (26) to his wife Mary Ann following their marriage on 15 June 1829 or, as already mentioned, a keepsake to mark the twenty-first birthday of Frances (Fanny) Kishere (31) which was celebrated a few weeks earlier than the incised date or, a very appropriate gift, handcrafted by William and Frances, in readiness for the sixtieth birthday of their father Joseph Kishere (8), in the spring of 1830. Regardless of its raison d'être, it will always be admired as a unique piece of Kishere stoneware.

Plate 51a. *A typical squat 'Dutch' shaped jug covered with vine leaves and grapes. Insdribed on the base 'Made by William Kishere Figured by Fanny Nov. 25 1829' (illustrated). H. 7¼in. (18.4cm) c.1805-10.* PRIVATE COLLECTION

REFERENCES AND SOURCES

CHAPTER 1
1. Leslie Freeman: *Going to the Parish – Mortlake and the Parish Church of St Mary the Virgin*, Barnes and Mortlake History Society, 1993.
2. Corporation of London, Records Office. Biographical details of Sir Brook Watson.
3. Edited by Sir Leslie Stephen and Sir Sidney Lee: *The Dictionary of National Biography, Vol. 1*, Oxford University Press, London: Humphrey Milford.
4. Arthur Bryant: *The Years of Endurance 1793-802*, Heron Books, London, 1942.
5. Sir Richard Phillips: *A Morning's Walk from London to Kew*, 1817.
6. C. Marshall Rose: *Nineteenth Century Mortlake and East Sheen*, privately printed, 1961.
7. Dr. David Redstone: 'William Sanders Mortlake Pottery 1745-1823', *English Ceramic Circle Transactions*, Vol. 17, Part 1.

★The Arabic numerals in parentheses refer to the family tree (pages 82-83).

General Sources
Edited by Kenneth O. Morgan: *The Oxford Illustrated History of Britain*, Oxford University Press, 1990.
Edward Wedlake Brayley, F.S.A.: *A Topographical History of Surrey*, David Bogue, Fleet Street, London, 1840.
David Gordon Wilson: *The Thames: Record of a Working Waterway*, B.T. Batsford Ltd., London, 1987.

CHAPTER 2
1. Frank Britton: *London Delftware*, Jonathan Horne, London, 1986.
2. *The Apprentices of Great Britain 1710-1782*, Public Record Office, Kew.
3. Dr. Bernard M. Watney: 'The Vauxhall China Works, 1751-1764', *English Ceramic Circle Transactions* Vol. 13, Part 3, 1989.
4. Roger Massey: 'Nicholas Crisp at Bovey Tracey', *English Ceramic Circle Transactions* Vol. 18, Part 1, 2002.
5. Charles Hailstone: 'Alleyways of Mortlake and East Sheen', Barnes and Mortlake History Society, 1983.
6. John Eustace Anderson: *A Short Account of the Mortlake Potteries*, printed privately, 1894 (Appendix 8).
7. Adrian Oswald in collaboration with R.J.C. Hildyard and R.G. Hughes: *English Brown Stoneware 1670-1900*, Faber and Faber, 1982.
8. Sir Richard Phillips: *A Morning's Walk from London to Kew*, 1817.

CHAPTER 3
1. J.F. Blacker: *The ABC of English Salt-Glaze Stoneware from Dwight to Doulton*, Stanley Paul & Co., London, 1922..
2. Frank and Janet Hamer: *The Potters Dictionary of Materials and Techniques*, A. & C. Black, London 1991 (third edition).
3. Peter Starkey: *Saltglaze*, Pitman Publishing Ltd., London, 1977.
4. Charles Hailstone: *Alleyways of Mortlake and East Sheen*, Barnes and Mortlake History Society, 1983.
5. A.R. Mountford, MA, FMA, FSA (General Editor): *Journal of Ceramic History*, No. 11, Denis Haselgrove and John Murray (Editors): 'John Dwight's Fulham Pottery 1672-1978. A collection of Documentary Sources', Stoke-on-Trent City Museums, 1979.
6. Desmond Eyles: *The Doulton Lambeth Wares*, Hutchinson & Co. (Publishers) Ltd., London 1975.
7. A. Aikin: *Illustrations of Arts and Manufactures*, John Van Voorst, London 1841.

General Sources
Wolf Mankowitz: *Wedgwood*, The Hamlyn Publishing Group Ltd., London, 1966.
Donald E. Frith: *Mold Making for Ceramics*, A. & C. Black (Publishers) Ltd., London, 1992.

CHAPTER 4
1. J.F. Blacker: *The ABC of English Salt-Glaze Stoneware from Dwight to Doulton*, Stanley Paul & Co., London, 1922, p.120.

CHAPTER 5
1. J.E. Anderson: *A Short Account of the Mortlake Potteries*, privately printed, 1894). See Appendix 7.
2. C. Marshall Rose: *Nineteenth Century Mortlake and East Sheen*, privately printed, 1961.
3. J.F. Blacker: *The ABC of English Salt-Glaze Stoneware from Dwight to Doulton*, Stanley Paul & Co., 1922.
4. The English Ambassador at the Hague persuaded John Ariens van Hamme to settle in this country and in October 1676 he was granted a patent for the exercise of his art for 'making tiles and porcelain and other earthenwares after the way practised in Holland, which hath not been practised in this our kingdom'.

General Sources
Details of baptisms and burials have been extracted from the Mortlake Parish Records held on microfilm at the Surrey History Centre, Woking.
Dates of death and ages at the time of death are to be found in the Mortlake Churchyard and Cemetery listings generously provided by the Barnes and Mortlake History Society.
The 9,000 index books at the General Register Office, Kingsway, London list all births, marriages and deaths registered in England and Wales since 1837. These volumes are compiled in quarters to March, June, September and December and quote only the name of the individual and the registration district. Where appropriate, full details have been obtained by ordering copies of the birth, death or marriage certificate.
The International Genealogical Index for London has been of some help in locating Kishere marriages and baptisms in the Parish Registers of London Churches. Both the I.G.I. and the Parish Records are held in the Westminster City Archives, St. Ann's Street, Westminster.

INDEX

The numbers in parenthesis following most of the Kishere names refer to the Family Tree on pages 81-83.
Page numbers in bold type refer to illustrations and captions.

Apart from a few exceptions, minor decorative sprigs e.g. hounds, riders, beaters, trees and so on, have not been included in these listings. The schedule of items and sprigs in John Anderson's stoneware collection (Appendix 8) and the catalogue of pottery in Mortlake Parish Church (Appendix 9) are treated as self-indexing and only entries of particular interest or relevance to the main text have been selected for the general index.

Drawn from Nature & on Stone by W. Westall A.R.A.

M O R T

London, Pub: by Rodwell & M.